STONE AGE
WISDOM

STONE AGE
WISDOM

The Healing Principles
of Shamanism

TOM CROCKETT

FAIR WINDS
PRESS
GLOUCESTER, MASSACHUSETTS

Text © 2003 by Tom Crockett

First published in the USA in 2003 by
Fair Winds Press
33 Commercial Street
Gloucester, MA 01930

Library of Congress Cataloging-in-Publication Data available

ISBN: 1-59233-014-2

10 9 8 7 6 5 4 3 2 1

Cover design by John Hall Design Group; www.johnhalldesign.com
Book design by Anne Gram

Printed and bound in Canada

ACKNOWLEDGMENTS

When I was in the process of writing this book, a wise woman asked me what I was writing about. I told her that I was writing about the spiritual wisdom and shamanic traditions of our Stone Age ancestors and how it might have relevance for us today. She seemed to think about this for a moment, then asked, "How do you research something like that?" The long answer is that you research it with books and the anthropological studies of hunter-gatherer cultures that still live in much the same ways that our Stone Age ancestors did, as well as with travel and imaginative leaps, and with long discussions with indigenous healers and urban contemporary shamans. The short answer is that you try to live it. Thanks, Mary.

To write a book about the wisdom traditions of our Stone Age ancestors without expressing gratitude for the line of my own ancestors would seem an embarrassing oversight. I'm here to struggle with issues of spirituality and balance in a modern world precisely because people before me lived and fought and loved and laughed and died and were filled with awe and wonder at the world around them. Consciousness researcher Etzel Cardena has speculated that the predisposition toward and perhaps even the calling to engage in things shamanic may be genetic and inherited, encoded in our DNA. If that is the case, my own Stone Age ancestors are even more responsible for this book.

This book also grew out of my interaction with some magical people. There is a web of sacred relationships underlying this project. Meredith Misek, despite what evidence I might have provided to dissuade her, has always believed in me. David Gordon, a therapist, dreamworker, and old friend, first helped me map out some of the ideas that have emerged in this book. My teacher, Don Oscar Miro-Quesada, helped me make sense of a world of traditional knowledge and not only opened the door to a path of healing, but pushed me through it, as well. My practicing urban contemporary shaman friends Joe Maiorano, Carl Hyatt, and Alex Stark have shared themselves as only those with open hearts can. Together, we wrestle with issues both personal and professional as we endeavor to walk this ancient walk in a contemporary world. For four years now, I have carried the ideas of shamanic dreamwork to the Association for the Study of Dreams with the help of my friends Stan Krippner, Maria Volchenko, and Sven Doehner.

My good friend Sven, a therapist and dreamworker from Mexico City, offered me an alchemical vessel in which to cook the ideas I'm elaborating on here. I owe him a debt of gratitude for connecting me to marvelous healers like Mónica Del Valle and Sandra Sofiati. He also introduced me to my Mexican "Dream Team" of indigenous healers: Sr. Enedino Hernandez, Leonor Martinez, and Santiago Ortela. These gifted healers accepted this urban gringo as an equal from the start, with no jealousy and with respect for the medicine I was able to carry. Sven took me deep into the heart of Mexico and showed me how the traditional and the modern might be bridged.

For several years I have been teaching and exploring these ideas with a Healing Circle in Virginia. Julie, Kim, Dana, Paul,

Linda, Cheryl, Mildred, Dave, Barbara, Amy, Devon, Brenda, Madeleine, and all those who have joined or will join the circle, thanks for your courage and your integrity.

My agent, Jane Dystel, who inherited me from another agent and probably was not sure what to do with me, carried the idea of this book to editor Holly Schmidt at Fair Winds Press. I owe the material form of this book to their belief in it.

I also owe a debt of gratitude to the teachers I have had in the nonmaterial world, especially the guide I know as Gray Morning Bear.

Finally, I must express gratitude to the woman who most shaped this book in its final form. Every idea in here has been held up to the light of a patient, compassionate, and beautiful healer. The gift Kelly Leigh has been to me is one of the ways I know that the universe is alive, conscious, dynamic, connected, and especially, responsive. Prayers are answered.

CONTENTS

I NVOCATION

I stand in the center, calling the sacred numbers.

0 for the space in between, the unseen world,
and the rainbow dragon, guardian of the gate.

1 for Creator Spirit,
the undifferentiated living field.

2 for the divine feminine and the divine masculine,
night and day, stillness and movement,
soul and spirit.

3 for the worlds above us, below us, and around us,
mind, heart, and body.

4 for the winds, north, south, east, and west,
before me, behind me, to my right, and to my left.

5 for the elements and their energies,
earth, water, air, fire, and ether.

MEDICINE REFLECTIONS
OF THE TWO BEARS

There are people who believe that shamanism is the
spiritual property of one culture.
I am grateful for the planetary legacy shamanic cultures
have preserved for us.
I'm wary of stealing their souls.

There are people who believe that shamanism can only be
useful in foreign places.
I find the need for shamans wherever I go.
A life without soul is as sad in the city as it is in the jungle.

There are people who believe that true shamans are
recognized by their communities.
I believe that shamans have always served communities.
The new shamans will have to remember how to create
communities.

There are people who believe that shamanism is only
authentic if it's your ancestral tradition.
I agree, but isn't shamanism everyone's ancestral tradition?
Didn't we all dance around the same fires?

There are people who believe that shamanism is dying out.
I believe that shamanism was with us from the beginning
and is with us still.
A lineage like that should not be underestimated.

There are people who believe their path is the only path.
If you've found a path of spirit that takes you where you
need to go, stay on it.
We'll all meet at the top of the mountain.

There are people who travel vast distances to experience
shamanism.
I want to know what you do when you come home.
Are your visions growing corn?

Spirit
and
Language

Verbal untruth has the power to render us neurotic.

The strain between what is said and what is known
to be real is a powerful cause of conflict.
Tension between reality and what is said about
reality becomes a matter of profound importance.

Hugh Brody,
The Other Side of Eden:
Hunters, Farmers, and the Shaping of the World

FOR A SECULAR CULTURE, ANY DISCUSSION of spirit is awkward. Alternative healers, indigenous medicine carriers, and practitioners of New Age therapies and philosophies often use the word spirit (or the plural, spirits), soul, spirit guides, angels, and energies interchangeably. Michael Harner, one of the guiding forces behind the contemporary resurgence of interest in shamanism, has written, "…when I speak of 'spirits,' it is because that is the way shamans talk within the system. To practice shamanism, it is unnecessary and even distracting to be preoccupied with achieving a scientific understanding of what 'spirits' may really represent and why shamanism works."

On the other hand, people who come to shamanism from urban contemporary cultures have often already been exposed to terms like spirit, soul, Great Spirit, spirit guides, power animals, angels, and so on. They may know or think they know what they mean when they use these terms, but as a teacher and a writer, I find it is helpful to be clear about what *I* mean when I use this language.

I cannot say that what I have experienced is the right way or the only way to know these things, but since what I write about and teach is based on my experience and my understanding, I think it is only fair to lay the blanket of what I believe on the ground upon which we will work.

I believe most spiritual traditions use cultural language to describe an energetic universe. That is a universe that is first and foremost an energetic template from which material conditions and forms arise. This energetic sea connects us all. It is what we are made of. It is what makes us. I believe that this energetic field is conscious. It is the great dreamer, or what the Aborigines call "the Dreaming." It is what Native Americans refer to as "Great Spirit" or, sometimes, just "Spirit." (I will refer to the undifferentiated form as Great Spirit or the Dreaming, so as not to confuse it with that part of the Great Spirit we all carry with us.) Great Spirit is constantly dreaming energy into material form. I don't believe I can know why it is dreaming what it is dreaming. The best I can hope for is to listen to what it is dreaming and to try to align with that.

Among the many things that I cannot know but do suspect, based on the wisdom of the stories of my ancestors, is why this conscious universal field or Great Spirit needs to differentiate into material forms. I think Great Spirit takes form to know itself. We know things by contrast. We know light only because we know darkness. We know warmth only because we know cold. We know joy because we know sadness. We know safety because we know fear. We know love because we know hate.

It seems to me that the element that is most common to creation stories from cultures around the world is the very division and separation we find mirrored in our own birth at a cellular level. We come into existence when a fertilized egg divides, subdivides, and subdivides again. The great creation stories tell us time and again about a universal field or force or Great Spirit that divides or gives birth to darkness and lightness, feminine and masculine, the mother and the father. It divides again into the elements of earth, water, air, and fire. Those elements combine and differentiate into stones, plants, trees, animals, and humans. These archetypal energies differentiate again into classes, races, and species, and within these categories we get individual expressions of these universal forces. We can experience the archetypal or spirit "Dog." We can also experience the more localized form as a German Shepherd or a specific dog we know as "King" or "Rex" or whatever name it answers to.

Here is where it gets tricky. We often use the words "spirit" and "soul" interchangeably. Anthropologists have combined and translated often subtly distinct definitions to mean either spirit or soul in a rather arbitrary fashion. Some cultures have evolved complex cosmologies around spirit and soul. Shamans tend to have a simpler view, but even that simplified view has become clouded by layers of cross-culturalism. It is hard, for instance, to separate out what the *curanderos* (or healers) of Central and South America believed before the forced introduction of colonial Catholicism, and it is difficult to know what the Stone Age shamans of the Himalayas believed before the overlay of Hindu and Buddhist thought.

Again, with the caveat that this is what I have been taught and what I have come to feel is right based on practical experience, I would like to suggest this understanding of spirit and soul. Everything is born or begins with both a spirit and a soul. Though I don't claim to know the big picture, I think everyone is born with a purpose. Malidoma Somé has written about the belief his fellow Dagara tribespeople hold: "Every person is sent to this outpost called Earth to work on a project that is intended to keep this cosmic order healthy. Any person that fails to do what he or she must do energetically stains the cosmic order."

The shamans of many cultures agree that souls come up from the lower world and spirits come down from the upper world to join in physical form in this, the middle world. At death, our individual spirits rejoin the undifferentiated universal force or field holding the memories and life experiences accumulated in the middle world. The soul returns to the lower world, nourishing the Earth Mother and losing itself in the primal life force.

Spirit is that part of you that is undying. It has been born again and again. Spirit is your connection to the archetypal Human Spirit, the archetypal Elemental Spirit, the divine Masculine and Feminine Spirits, and to Great Spirit itself. Spirit is in no hurry for you to do anything. Spirit is pleased by balance and order. Without Spirit, your body dies, but death is simply part of the cycle to Spirit.

Soul, on the other hand, carries your sense of purpose and your power. Great Spirit dreamed you into existence for a reason— your soul's mission or destiny. Your soul has a sense of urgency about this mission because your soul is only with you for this turn of the wheel. It is your uniqueness, your gifts, your circumstances, and your potential—all the things you may or may not have with you the next time your spirit takes physical form. Soul loves adventure, excitement, passion, and creation. It wants to experience everything there is to feel while it has the gift of physical form. Soul will vex you if you ignore your purpose. It will do whatever it takes to get your attention. But even if you are paying attention, it's no guarantee that soul will not jump you off the deep end if it furthers your purpose for being born. While you cannot live without spirit, you can live without most of your soul, though the quality of that life would be severely compromised.

For shamans and shamanic healers, soul loss is one of the most common maladies. Soul has the capacity to fragment or, in a different language, soul energy can be depleted. It is quite natural to lose soul pieces or access to soul energy on a regular basis. Most of the time we recover from these little losses without any outside assistance. Soul loss occurring in childhood, before a strong sense of self has been developed, often needs outside help, as does soul loss occurring from serious life-threatening or emotional trauma.

Traditionally, we can experience soul loss in one of four ways. *Soul fright* occurs with serious violent trauma, such as a rape or beating in which we fear for our life. *Soul flight* occurs in near-death experiences when the soul comes too close to the other side and not all of the soul returns. Soul flight often occurs during accidents or surgery under the influence of anesthetics, and sometimes under the influence of plant spirit medicine when a proper guide for the experience is not present. Soul flight can also be accompanied by or confused with soul fright. *Soul theft* occurs when our soul energy is taken by another. Contemporary psychological explanations of soul theft suggest that soul energy can't be stolen, but that we give it away subconsciously. I believe that this does happen, usually as the result of a kind of low-grade but long-term abuse or a dramatic power imbalance in a relationship, but I also believe, as do traditional shamans, that others can steal our soul energy. This again is tricky for a lot of New Age believers. They want to believe that people can be healed by others from a distance and sometimes without their knowledge, but they are uncomfortable with the reverse position, that people can be harmed energetically from a distance. I think that to accept the possibility of one you have to accept the possibility of the other. Finally, the fourth kind of soul loss, *soul wandering*, occurs when we constantly repress the messages from our soul, refusing to remember our soul purpose on Earth. This is essentially choosing to live in a soul-deadening way.

Soul fright, soul flight, and soul theft are situations that require the attention of a skilled shaman or shamanic practitioner. This work should never be entered into lightly. If someone tells you that you need a soul retrieval, ask him to be specific about what he feels is wrong. The level of soul energy a shaman or shamanic practitioner is retrieving for you and the amount of time you've been without it can have significant repercussions in your life. Suddenly having your soul energy back can take some getting used to.

Soul wandering is really the area this book addresses. I believe that while many of us are walking around with soul loss or soul energy depletion due to soul fright, flight, or theft, most of the damage to our souls is the result of how we choose to live our lives. Learning to live with a shamanic worldview and reinvigorating our lives with the five principles that our Stone Age ancestors lived by means returning to alignment with our soul's purpose.

While it has been important for me to lay this groundwork, especially since it might differ from what you've learned elsewhere, it is not necessary for you to believe what I'm telling you in order to benefit from this book. As a matter of fact, I would prefer that you not "believe" anything I say. I want you to put it into practice and come to know it. If your cosmology differs from mine, that's fine. If your understanding of spirit and soul or a universal life force is different, that's fine, too. This work is too important to argue over the details.

When I conduct a ceremony, I do so with certain directions, such as north, south, east, and west, representing certain energies and elemental forces. I do this the way I was taught and the way that I have come to feel makes the most sense to me—it is a way that works. When I'm invited to participate in the ceremonies of others, I respect *their* traditions. If the elements and energies— the living forces—are invoked and honored, I don't care what positions they are placed in. And if the elements and energies are not invoked and honored, I silently invoke them myself.

You do not need to believe in spirits to read and benefit from this book, though I agree with therapist and author Arnold Mindell when he writes, "I have seen in my practice how many shamanic abilities appear when you stop doubting the reality of the spirit." All that really matters for us to move forward is an understanding that this book and this work is written from the perspective that the physical form the universe takes is based on an energetic or spiritual template. We can try to ignore this template or pattern, but we cannot separate from it. When we do not align ourselves with what is being dreamed, we become confused, lost, or disoriented. When we reject what is being dreamed, we become ill or suffer emotional or mental breakdowns. When we engage the energetic pattern of Spirit actively, we begin to live our soul's purpose.

This template is what is referred to as the world of spirit or the unseen world, but here, again, words fail us. Calling this template the unseen world is not entirely accurate. We do see this world in our dreams, in our visionary experiences, and at liminal moments manifesting in the physical world. Calling one world dreaming and one waking is problematic as well, because it is a distinction many cultures question—which world is the dream? Even referring to one world as the spirit world and one as the material world seems to suggest that they are separate, when, in fact, they are inextricably interconnected. Still, we have to use some kind of distinction, and I will use all of these names interchangeably with the understanding that none of them is completely correct.

We can learn to see, hear, or become aware of the unseen world the way our ancestors did. We can learn to see energetically, to understand our dreams, to engage spirit in dialogue, and to shift our energy. But more than just becoming aware of the energetic pattern upon which our physical existence is based, for this is not simply a guide to improving your intuition, we must learn to interact with this template through ceremony, embodied prayer, and creative action. The spirit world takes forms that are influenced by culture and personal experience, but it is as real as the material world.

The Art
of Balance

The knowledge that marks hunter-gatherers'
relationship to their territories is an intricate
mixture of the real and the supernatural.
There are facts about things and facts about spirits.
And the wall between these two kinds of entities is
not solid. People can cross from the natural to the
supernatural; spirits can move into the human
domain. Just as this divide between physical and
metaphysical is permeable, so also is the boundary
between humans and animals. In this way, the
boundaries around the human world are porous.
This porosity is the way of seeing and understanding
the world that underlies shamanism.

Hugh Brody,
The Other Side of Eden:
Hunters, Farmers, and the Shaping of the World

CHRISTINA SITS ACROSS FROM ME ON THE FLOOR. Candles flicker in
the darkened room. The smell of sage and copal incense wafts up

from a burner. Between us is an altar of stones, shells, feathers, and sacred tools gathered from around the world. It takes no special gift to see the exhaustion and pain in her eyes. She is embarrassed to be seeking spiritual counsel from a shamanic practitioner, but her embarrassment reveals how desperate she is. She tells me why she has come to me. She is not sick, but not well either. Doctors can find nothing wrong with her, but she feels like she has barely enough energy—enough life force—to get out of bed in the morning. She feels disconnected and afraid. She is married and has a beautiful son, a good job, material comfort, and yet something is missing. I close my eyes as I listen to her talk. I can both hear and see her more clearly with my eyes closed. Finally, she finishes talking and asks if I can help her. I answer her gently. Yes, I can help in the short term. I can work with her to heal the places from where her energy is leaking. I can help her recover the missing soul stuff without which she will not feel whole. The real healing, however, will come only with her decision to return to balance in her life—a path for which I might offer some guidance, but a path she alone has to walk.

What does it mean to live in balance?

We know what it feels like to live out of balance. It may begin as a nagging sense of dis-ease or discomfort—a lack of energy or enthusiasm for life. We should be happy, but we don't feel happy. We have the things popular culture tells us we need in order to be fulfilled, and yet we aren't. We ask the kinds of questions that are hard to answer. Why am I here? Why is this happening to me? Is there something I'm missing? Sometimes we don't discover how out of balance we are until the consequences rear up like a mythical serpent and manifest in our lives as physical illness, the emotional pain of failed relationships, spiritual crisis, or mental breakdown. We've lost the sense of the world as a living, animate web of relationships, and it is this fundamental imbalance that is fueling our search for spiritual meaning through healing therapies, indigenous wisdom traditions, established world religions, and New Age spiritual eclecticism.

Being out of balance means not being in a reciprocal relationship with the world of spirit. We know this deep inside. It is why we turn to spiritual traditions for answers. When we are out of balance with the unseen world of spirit, energy, and life force, we cannot be in balance in the physical and material world. The world of spirit is a template upon which the physical, temporal world manifests. When we align with spirit we are "plugged in" to an infinite source of energy. We have a purpose and a mission. We wake up grateful for being alive, grateful for the people around us, and blessed by the experiences that come to us. Most of us have felt this way for short periods of time in our lives. It is the feeling people describe after surviving near-death experiences. Being in balance means living this reality as the rule, rather than the exception.

Our relationship with the world of spirit affects every part of our lives: our personal relationships with family, friends, and community; our relationship with money, power, material possessions, and the work we do in the world; and our relationship with spirit, death, and the natural world of cycles and change. When we live in a way that's closed to the possibility of everything but what our most mundane senses tell us, we miss the real nature of our problems. We don't realize that the argument we've been having with our mother for years seems so intractable because we are both caught in an energetic field that has very specific roles that need to be played. We may feel unwell without being able to really see the toxicity in our own environment. We may feel unfulfilled, while at the same time ignoring the soul messages that are trying to lead us toward fulfillment. We may consume the resources of the planet voraciously without realizing that we are despoiling our own bed. Our ability to open up to an unseen world of spirit and energy is critical.

When we do not have enough energy or power coming to us from a spiritual source, we try to take it from others by coercion, manipulation, or force. We try to buy and barter for more energy. We know we need something, but what we don't know is how to find it authentically. And, while it is to be expected that we will occasionally lose our sense of connection to spirit in the act of living our lives, we were not meant to make that imbalance a way of life.

There is no quick fix to this situation. No guru or spiritual leader can benevolently grant us a sense of balance. Returning to wholeness in our relationships is life work. One way that we can return to balance is to look backward for a spiritual practice that not only honors the "aliveness" of things, but also offers practical techniques for engaging with the unseen world. Shamanism is such a practice. It may have been the progenitor of all our spiritual practices. Its techniques for altering perception to include the unseen world are hardy enough to have survived from the Paleolithic era and vital enough to have remained the physical or spiritual intervention of choice for many people around the world today. For a culture that honors progress and looking forward, this may seem like an odd prescription, but if we can find the wisdom to heal our bodies in Paleolithic diets, why not wisdom to heal our souls in Paleolithic spiritual practices? We must, however, be careful of superficially embracing the shamanic cultural traditions of any particular tribal or indigenous people. To return to balance we must redefine and recreate a spiritual practice for people living urban contemporary lives. *Stone Age Wisdom* is a guide to a new expression of an ancient tradition.

This is not a book of easy answers. Living a life based on shamanic principles of respect, awareness, and sacred reciprocity is not easy. Following this path is not a guarantee of peace and harmony. Ecstasy, bliss, peace, and happiness are things we all have a right to experience, but they are not what life is. They are the valleys that come between the hills of stress and challenge. Balance is a dynamic process. Balance is not necessary when we are lying on our backs, when we are stuck, still, or dead. Balance is important when we are moving, dancing, riding the wave. Balance is what we lose and struggle to find when we make the descent to do soul work. If we have the techniques and the energy to regain our balance, we are that much stronger or wiser the next time we find ourselves riding the wave of change.

Stone Age people left no written records of what they believed. What we do know is that they were hunters and gatherers. One way of trying to understand the worldview of our Stone Age ancestors is to look at the beliefs of contemporary hunter-gatherer cultures. We find such cultures existing—much the same as they have for thousands of years—in places like the Arctic north, the rain forests of the Amazon, and the deserts of southern Africa and Australia. These indigenous tribal cultures experience a world of both seen and unseen forces. A bear, goose, salmon, or snake may at once be a messenger from the unseen world—a representative of the universal essence of bear, goose, salmon, or snake—and a source of food. A tree is both a source of firewood or construction material and the container for a conscious spirit. A stone in a sling may kill a rabbit to feed a family. A stone in a fire—baked to a white heat for a sweat lodge—may sing a song of power. A stone in a medicine pouch may be used to draw off fever or negative energy. These things are alive in every sense of the word.

We've lost this sense of the "aliveness" of things. We had to sacrifice it in order to achieve the technological advances of modern life. But it is precisely this loss that makes our "triumphs" over the material world so hollow and, in the end, unsatisfying. We grant the attribute of "life" to animals and, grudgingly, to plants, but only in a hierarchical sense that would surely exclude them from any country club of which we humans were members. We are even more reserved when it comes to acknowledging consciousness in things around us. Hence we've dreamed a world for ourselves in which we are alone and disconnected. The decisions we make out of such a dream are the self-centered decisions of children. We expect to be served, to have our needs met, and to see our wants instantly gratified. We plunder the natural world and consume voraciously, but we're never really satisfied.

This blindness to spirit, to the animated, conscious, dynamic, interconnected, and responsive nature of the world around us, is the fundamental imbalance that we face as we enter the third millennium. We know at some deep level that there is more to the world than what we perceive with our physical senses, but the ability to navigate in and interact with this unseen world is something we've devalued and suppressed. We can only really return to balance by acknowledging and experiencing this animated, unseen world and beginning to make our choices from this awareness.

Another way to work toward a return to balance is to understand that every interaction occurs within an underlying energetic field. Our ego-centered view of most problems or conflicts is that they are caused by people. We believe that if we fix the other or if we fix ourselves, we will fix the field. This is the psychological explanation. The shamanic explanation is that the field comes first. The potential for conflict and the roles within that conflict exist apart from the people who might currently be hosting or advocating for a particular position. Arnold Mindell writes in *The Leader as Martial Artist*, "In many parts of the world, human problems are understood to be a consequence of force fields and spirits and therefore require the work of shamans to be healed…. If we perceive the field as being the primary force behind all things, we develop shamanism." Energetic fields don't get fixed. If we become aware of them and engage them consciously, we can learn from them and then step out of them, but working the field requires attention to more than just the person or persons within it. We need to consider the dream or purpose of the field itself. An awareness of underlying energetic fields is one of the skills we turn to our Stone Age ancestral tradition of shamanism to develop.

The subtitle of this book, *The Healing Principles of Shamanism*, is not an idea I take lightly. It is my belief that the world needs more shamans. Not Shamans with a capital S, but shamans as individuals who carry the wisdom of a hunter-gatherer's relationship to place, community, and spirit in their hearts. As individuals, as communities, as cultures, and as a planet, we are living lives out of balance. We know this deep in our hearts, either because we've glimpsed a more fulfilling vision of what life might be like or because we are painfully aware of an emptiness that no amount of material success can fill.

It is important to me that I also make clear a distinction: Engaging in an urban contemporary spiritual practice based on the principles of shamanism is not the same thing as becoming a shaman. Over the past fourteen years I have met, worked with, studied with, and apprenticed to people I consider to be shamans, *curanderos,* and medicine carriers of various cultural traditions. I have participated in indigenous healing ceremonies and had personal experiences that were miraculous. I have been of service as a healer and a shamanic counselor, and as a teacher of shamanic techniques and traditions. I am comfortable with the label "shaman" or "shamanic counselor" only in the sense of a job description—it accurately describes the service I perform in my community.

I also know that the wisdom and the dedication of some of the traditional shamans I have had the honor of meeting is something that I will probably not attain in my lifetime. My work and my calling is here, and that work, while based on principles I deeply believe in, looks different than other traditional forms of shamanic practice because it is evolving in an urban contemporary environment.

I have tried to make this book both inspirational and practical. It includes exercises that open the door to the world of spirit. You'll learn ways to seek answers and be open to guidance from spirit. You'll learn to dance with change rather than fight it. You'll learn how simple ceremonies and rituals can heal old emotional wounds, attract prosperity and positive energy, and help you face life's challenges. And you'll experience the ecstasy of spirit moving through you when you begin to live your dream. Shamanism has many definitions because shamans often perform a variety of functions in their communities. I believe, however, that there are some core practices in shamanism that are especially useful to urban contemporary practitioners. I have used these core practices to organize this book. Urban contemporary shamans and those pursuing a spiritual or healing path based on the principles of shamanism need to know how to:

DREAM—to be open to and to understand the wisdom of the Dreaming;

VISION-SHIFT—to develop the ability to sense that everything is alive;

JOURNEY—to enter into dialogue with spirit;

SHAPE-SHIFT—to practice the art of change;

CONDUCT RITUALS—to mediate between the seen and the unseen worlds;

DREAM-WEAVE—to direct will and intention through embodied prayer and creative action.

Each one of these topics could easily take up a whole book, but my intention is not to explore each practice exhaustively. I am interested in demonstrating how they might weave together into an urban contemporary spiritual practice, so I will introduce each practice with some simple exercises. See "Resources" on page 266 for more in-depth study of each of the topics.

My task is to open the door to a new possibility and give you enough help to begin to experience spirit directly. While I don't mean to suggest that any spiritual practice is or should be easy, I have found that once people experience the unseen world for themselves, the shift that occurs is both profound and long-lasting. What I want you to take away from this book is your own very personal glimpse of the unseen world.

The Urban Contemporary Shaman

*When shamans talk of other worlds, they do not mean
that these are disconnected from this world.
Rather, these worlds represent the true nature of
things and the true causes of events in this world.
The understanding is widely shared in the
community, and many people may be shamans
to a greater or lesser degree, according to their
insight into this reality.*

Piers Vitebsky,
*The Shaman: Voyages of the Soul Trance, Ecstasy,
and Healing
from Siberia to the Amazon*

AN HOUR INTO A CROSS-COUNTRY flight from California to Virginia, after the complimentary beverage and peanuts, after the in-flight movie, after the lowering of the cabin lights so that my fellow passengers could settle into their pillows and blankets, I leaned against the bulkhead and looked out into the clear night sky. My parallel lives as a corporate consultant and a shamanic teacher require this kind of travel on a regular basis. Sometimes impatient with the speed of mere physical air travel, I combine it with spiritual air travel to make better use of my time. I pulled my CD player from my bag and slipped the headphones over my ears. The drumming CD in the player is not what most people would call music. Even fans of percussion would find the repetitive driving beat of a single drum boring beyond belief. But then that's the point. Stripped of anything that might be described as a distraction, the single drum beat entrains my brain's frequency, shifting my consciousness to a deep meditative state in much the same way that my ancient tribal ancestors were affected by the drums and rattles that resonated around their campfires. In this relaxed but conscious state of awareness, on the edge of dreaming, the hard edges of waking reality soften and blur, revealing another world—a world of spirit, story, magic, energetic templates, and maps.

So here I was, flying in one of the twentieth century's most amazing technologies while simultaneously flying by one of the Paleolithic era's most enduring technologies—the shamanic trance journey. The technique of trance journeying has been passed down from the very dawn of time. It has, at various times and in various cultures, been facilitated by drumming, dancing, meditative practices, sacred posture, plant spirit sacraments, fasting, and ritual. While it may sound exotic, it is no stranger than the various meditative practices we have embraced in the West. It is, in fact, very much like meditation. Both meditation and trance journeying employ an altered state of consciousness, but where meditation seeks stillness, trance journeying is an active process.

It is practiced by shamans, healers, and visionaries, but it is also used by ordinary individuals seeking spiritual guidance, balance, and a way to align themselves with the unseen world. Today we may try to explain the effects of trance journeying physiologically or psychologically, but that does not negate the fundamental power of the experience any more than psychological or physiological explanations lessen the immediacy of a powerful dream. Trance journeying is not difficult to do. Most people can learn to have successful, if not amazing, experiences. Trance journeying, however it is induced, is a primal technology for engaging the unseen or subtle worlds.

To travel in unseen realms is both an inner and an outer journey. It is a movement inside our own soul landscapes and an exploration of worlds that exist outside of our perceptual framework. As the drumming carried me, I slipped from my body and passed ghostlike through the metal skin of the plane. I became aware of my body transforming. I felt the lift of air currents under new wings. I became a creature of the air. I was only lightly in the trance state at that time, still aware of being in two places at once. I was both inside the plane, shoulder to shoulder with a dozing real estate agent from San Francisco, and outside the plane, winging through the night sky in the body of a hawk. As a hawk I was aware of the cold and the altitude, but they were not things I had to control. Looking over at the jet, I could see myself leaning against the window, eyes closed, fogging the inner pane briefly with each long, slow exhalation. Within the plane, my physical body was constrained and defined by the principles of physical reality. Outside the plane, time and space were merely suggestions, not rules.

I left the plane to fly off into the night. I knew I could return to it in an instant, but now I had another journey to make.

Journeying can work as an open-ended exploration. Traditional shamans journey both to commune with the spirits—to establish positive relationships and explore the territory of the spirit world—and to solve specific problems or find answers to questions. I have always found it much more effective to journey with a purpose and a question. I was looking for a solution—a solution to the problem of balance.

Everywhere I look, I see the effects of a culture out of balance. As a healer, I know first-hand that my clients suffer from imbalance. As a teacher, my young students are already painfully aware of how far out of balance their parents' lives are. Something about our way of being in the world is working against our desire for peace, happiness, and fulfillment. I believe that this imbalance is a matter of spirit. Our denial of spirit—of anything we cannot see, touch, taste, hear, or feel—cuts us off from the one thing that could bring us into a balanced relationship with the planet, with each other, and with ourselves. Many people are turning to religion for answers, but there are elements of most of the world's dominant religions that seem to be working to keep us from finding true balance.

True balance, as I understand it, is harmony between the seen and the unseen forces—between the spirit and the material. It is congruence between the conscious and the unconscious. Attending to one without attending to the other causes imbalance. Pursuing spirit and ignoring the material world is the mystic's path, the path of the hermit, the monk, or the recluse. It does not speak to the lives most of us lead. But to ignore spirit in favor of the material is to ignore the map by which our waking reality manifests. We stumble about, making decisions and choices with no guidance, no sense of the sacred quality of life. So, where should we turn for a model of living in balance? I suspected that the answer was in our past.

As a species, we have spent the vast majority of our time on this planet as hunters and gatherers. As hunter-gatherers, we lived stable existences. We were both nomadic and yet tied to the land. Our Stone Age ancestors had skills and abilities that still exist in the remaining hunting and gathering cultures of the world. The Amazonian, Aboriginal, and Arctic hunter-gatherer tribes live in what we might call a state of material poverty and spiritual abundance. I wonder how they would characterize us? The Australian Aboriginal wisdom keepers maintain that the modern world is out of alignment because, in our pursuit of material things, we have forgotten our spiritual obligation to dream the world into existence. The shift to an agricultural society required a shift in values, by which we negated many of the life-affirming principles of our hunter-gatherer ancestors. I know that we cannot return to some idealized notion of our hunter-gatherer past, but it seems to me that there may be answers for us there.

And what better way to access the wisdom of our hunter-gatherer ancestors than by their own Paleolithic technology—the shamanic trance journey? I knew from experience that I could move forward and backward in time while journeying, though time in the spirit world is often an ambiguous concept. I had read and studied the shamanic traditions of a wide range of hunter-gatherer cultures and so could not help coming into contact with their cosmologies, philosophies, and ways of being. I had apprenticed with teachers of shamanic cultures. I was not engaging in this work blindly. I knew, or strongly suspected, that the answer I was looking for would be found in our past, and journeying was a way to get there. For some people, a shamanic trance journey may seem like an exercise in fantasy, self-delusion, or wishful thinking. But I knew from repeated personal experience that this simple but powerful technique allowed me to access information for which I had no rational way of accounting. I know my own imagination. I know what it feels like to invent in my mind. I know how long it takes. The information that comes to me in a shamanic trance journey comes too quickly, is too complete, and resonates with reality in a way that is far wiser than I am capable of inventing. I was convinced that the answer to the problem of balance in contemporary life was to be found in the Stone Age spiritual path of shamanism.

For 10 years I'd pursued a personal spiritual quest into ancient and contemporary practices of shamanism. The principles of this practice had affected every aspect of my life. They had dragged me, at times kicking and screaming, into a process of balancing. I had taught shamanic techniques. I had worked as a shamanic counselor and healer. I had written and created from a place I consider shamanic. I had championed the adaptation and refinement of an urban contemporary practice of shamanism through books and newsletters. But there was still something I was missing. There was a piece to this puzzle that I did not yet understand. I knew how powerful shamanic principles had been in my life and I knew how much they had affected those I taught and counseled, but becoming a shaman was certainly not a path open to everyone. Could people adopt a shamanic way of being without becoming shamans? How might the healing and balancing principles of a shamanic worldview reach a wider audience? How might I best share the wisdom of a shamanic worldview with a new audience?

The word shaman comes to us from the Evenk, a small group of hunters and reindeer herders in Siberia, and there are many definitions for "shamans." It literally means "one who can see in the dark," or "master of fire." The Siberian herders used the word *saman* to describe people who were able to journey out of their bodies on behalf of the tribe—influencing the spirits of weather, communing with the ancestors, and interceding with the animal spirits on behalf of hunters. Shamans were and are the spiritual specialists in their communities. In a remarkably short period of time, the word shaman came to be used by anthropologists around the world to describe similar practitioners. The similarities in shamanic techniques and worldviews between people who had had no previous contact were amazing and probably contributed to the word shaman coming into general usage. The anthropologist and scholar Mercea Eliade called shamans "technicians of ecstasy." They were described as sorcerers by the Jesuit priests exploring the New World and as charlatans and tricksters by the missionaries and scientists who came later. They were considered to be both mentally ill and to be the equivalent of Stone Age psychiatrists by the different researchers who encountered them. In truth, even today the shaman may seem to be a priest, a visionary, a psychologist, an oracle, a teacher, a healer, a magician, a charlatan, an artist, or a storyteller, depending on which role he or she is currently playing for the community. A shaman seems illusive because he or she is constantly shape-shifting to better serve the healing that needs to occur.

The best definition of a shaman I have found is "one who uses out-of-body journeys to mediate between the seen and the unseen worlds on behalf of individuals or communities." The two elements of this definition—the out-of-body journey and the act of mediation—are essential. While shamans do heal with other modalities, it is the out-of-body journey that is universally shamanic. And while it is possible to learn the techniques of out-of-body travel, the ability or propensity to make such journeys is not in itself shamanic. A shaman serves spirit, community, and individual. The shaman mediates between the material world and the spirit world. Usually this mediation takes the form of balancing seen and unseen forces, making propitiatory offerings, recovering lost soul parts, or conducting healing ceremonies. Shamans are the expert navigators of the spirit realms. There are traditional and contemporary shamans who continue this way of working around the world today. They may have apprenticed with indigenous wisdom teachers or studied shamanism through a contemporary shamanic training program, but they serve individuals and communities and continue the lineage of their Stone Age ancestors. Whether they call themselves shamans or shamanic practitioners or shamanic counselors, you are probably closer to a shaman than you think.

But there is also a growing spiritual movement that is embracing what I would call a shamanic worldview. They may never choose to do the work of a shaman for individuals and communities, but they do understand the fundamental beauty of the guiding principles a shaman or shamanic practitioner lives by. To return to the quote that opened this chapter, when Piers Vitebsky writes, "The understanding is widely shared in the community, and many people may be shamans to a greater or lesser degree, according to their insight into this reality," I think he is describing not only traditional shamanic cultures, but also what is happening in our own. Perhaps adopting the worldview and guiding principles that inform a shaman's reality is becoming a shaman to a "lesser degree" based on "insight into this reality."

Adopting those principles and bringing them into our lives might help us find the balance of which we are sorely in need. My quest, the reason I was making this journey out of my body, was to find answers to my questions.

What are the core principles of a shamanic worldview?

How might I communicate them simply and without reference to a specific culture?

How could I make these principles come alive through experiential practice?

Hawk awareness returned to me. I felt the chill of the wind. I looked down.

I have always been fascinated by pristine and primal landscapes. For brief moments, short stretches of flying time, one crosses places in the western part of the United States that appear, at least from the air, unmarked by human habitation and exploration. By night this is a land without streetlights or the headlamps of automobiles. This was the land I was flying over now, both by jet and as the spirit of a hawk, so the lone sparkle of light below caught my attention immediately. I was drawn down to it. I circled down, spiraling toward the light. The light became a campfire. The smell of sage and sweet herbs wafted up from the fire. I glided easily onto the low branch of pinion pine on the side of the fire opposite an old man. He had the look of a Native American, an elder, with gray hair braided back and a bearskin blanket drawn around his shoulders. He was singing a droning rhythmic chant as he tossed pinches of dried herbs from a leather pouch onto the fire.

He seemed to know I was there, for while he did not look directly at me, he did stop his song and begin to speak. At first, they were just syllables, sounds I could not understand, but gradually, as he spoke, I found that I could understand him.

"Spirit, do you come from yesterday or tomorrow?" I thought about this for a moment. I had no doubt that he was addressing me. I assumed that I had traveled back in time, so I was coming from his tomorrow, but I had no way of knowing this for sure. Even if I had known for sure, however, I seemed to have no way of answering as the hawk.

"No matter," he continued, "I know you are here because of my dream." He turned back to the fire and tossed another pinch of sage onto some of the glowing coals. He seemed lost in thought for a long time, and I found myself studying the fire.

"I dreamed of a time long past or long to come," he began, "a great age of miracles and wonders, a time when the people commanded the power of earth, air, fire, and water. A time of stone and iron and great movement. A time of quickness and many voices. But this was also a time of great sadness and confusion. The people had lost their ability to dream true. They grew apart from their plant sisters and animal brothers. They forgot to give thanks to the Earth Mother and the Sky Father. They grew blind to the tree spirits and forgot the language of the stone people. They even forgot their relationship to one another. They had no tribes and no nations, except when they came together in hatred to make war. Each man became a tribe unto himself, each woman a village of one, alone and separate. Is this the time you come from?" He asked this last question without looking up at me, but I knew that it was me he was addressing.

Was this my time? In many ways it sounded true to my world. We controlled the natural environment in ways that would have seemed unthinkable 200 years before. We built bridges across great bodies of water, controlled rivers with dams and locks. We tunneled through the Earth and took great quantities of minerals from her belly. We harnessed fire to forge metal and to thrust ourselves into the sky. We moved at great speeds, and our technologies carried the voices of many. And yes, we had isolated ourselves from the elements with which we had once sought to live in harmony. We saw ourselves as separate from the other life forms on the planet. We even grew isolated from each other.

I came not from a place of despair, though, but from a place of hope. The people I knew, the children and adults of my world, were also hungry for something they knew was missing from their lives. All the material success was not bringing the happiness we had supposed it would. We were searching for a way of being that returned spirit and relationship, connection and community to our lives.

I spread my wings and formed the words, "Yes, the time you speak of is the world from which I have journeyed."

"Then you have come for the Five Stones," he answered. I was aware that he must have heard me. I was relieved to find that I could communicate with him.

"The Five Stones?" I asked.

"The Five Stones are what my people stand on. They are what we build upon. The Five Stones give the two-leggeds a place among all the other animals. With the Five Stones, we have a way of being in the world that is both balanced and active. The Five Stones teach us the laws by which we take right action in the world."

I thought about what he had said. Were there five truths that transcended culture and time? Was this the wisdom of my ancestors?

"Can you take another form?" he asked. I knew I could take any form I chose when I journeyed, but sometimes getting from one form to another took me a moment. This time, however, the shift was seamless. One moment I was perched high in a pinion pine, the next moment I was seated on the ground beside the old man. He did not turn to acknowledge my presence, though I knew he was aware of me. It did not seem rude; rather, it seemed polite, as if looking a spirit in the eye would have been bad manners.

"You see," he began without preamble, "My people say Grandmother Spider dreams the world into existence. They say that she pulls a living spirit from the great sky and drops it into the world." The old man smoothed out a space in the white ash in front of him. He made a single dot with a steady index finger in the ash.

"This is the First Stone," he explained. "That everything in the world is alive. All things come from spirit. When Grandmother Spider gathers up a spirit or a life force from the heavens, she rolls it into a beautiful ball of shimmering white threads. As it drops into the world, it takes some physical form: a seed, a stone, an egg. It is born in physical form. Sometimes that spirit has a short life-time to live its purpose and to be of service. Things that move the quickest and have the most freedom tend to live short and fast lives. Rooted things, like trees and mountains, live the longest. They are the ancestors. Do you understand the First Stone?"

"Yes," I nodded, "that everything in the world is alive, that we are all the dream of Grandmother Spider." I made a dot in the earth in front of me.

"Is this a difficult truth or an easy one?" he asked.

"It was not a truth I was raised with, but one I have adopted. In that sense it is not an easy truth, but it is one I practice. For many of the people of my time, it is certainly a difficult truth. We are taught that life—aliveness—is a gift reserved for people, animals, and plants."

He seemed to consider this. He took his finger and carefully traced a circle about 10 inches in diameter around his first dot. "This is the Second Stone," he explained. "When Grandmother Spider drops a living spirit into the world, it falls into a pool of awareness. This pool is consciousness. As everything falls into this pool, everything is conscious. Everything is alive and everything is conscious."

This made sense to me. It resonated with what I had learned from different teachers on my spiritual path. It was in alignment with my own experiences encountering spirit. "How is consciousness different from being alive?" I asked.

"Alive is the spark, the glowing ember that produces heat." He jabbed at the fire with a stick, stirring coals as he spoke. "It is the seed, the animating force. Consciousness is presence, it is awareness. All things are alive or they are not. A thing cannot be partially alive. We believe that sometimes the alive spirit of a person, plant, animal, or stone leaves its container behind and goes in search of a new container, but it is always best to treat a thing as if it were alive, in the same way that it is polite to approach a lodge as if someone were inside it. Consciousness comes in degrees. We cannot be partially alive, but we can be partially conscious. The consciousness of stones is not lesser in degree than the consciousness of people, but it is a slower awareness. We are often too impatient to listen to stones."

I drew a circle around my own dot. "So everything is alive and everything is conscious."

"Yes, these are the First and Second Stones. The First Stone teaches us to listen, to observe, to pay attention to everything. It teaches us vigilance. We learn to watch everything as everything watches us. The Second Stone teaches us respect and to walk gently in the world. If everything is conscious, we must be aware that ours are not the only desires that matter."

He drew a series of concentric circles around the original dot but within the larger circle representing the pool of consciousness. "The Third Stone is the lesson of transformation and movement. Everything is meant to move and to change. When Grandmother Spider drops a seed of life into the pool of consciousness, it creates ripples, waves, like a pebble dropped in still water. Those waves affect every other living, conscious element in the world. We know we are in motion from the very beginning of our existence in material form. People age, plants grow, rivers change their course, oceans reshape their shorelines, mountains dissolve to grains of sand, and grains of sand compress to form great slabs of stone waiting to be thrust up into mountains once again. The only thing we can rely on is that we are constantly moving. We are meant to change and transform. Transformation defines us; to fight change is to deny our very nature."

I thought about this one for a moment. The Third Stone, it seemed to me, might be the most difficult truth of my time. The world around us seems to be changing so fast that we seek stability by trying to deny or control the pace of change. Because we trust in nothing we cannot see, hear, smell, taste, or touch, change seems a frightening thing. We do not surrender to change, navigating it, surfing it, and adapting to new conditions. We fight change. We look for people to blame when change threatens our comfort. We have gotten so good at resisting change and we spend so much energy avoiding it that when change is finally thrust upon us, it is usually dramatic and overwhelming.

"The Fourth Stone is relationship," he continued. This time he drew two lines bisecting the circle and forming a cross intersecting at the center point he first drew. "Because Grandmother Spider dropped us all into the great pool of consciousness, we are each connected and in sacred relationship to every other seed of life. We are swimming in the same pool of consciousness. How can we not be connected?"

"I believe my people once knew the truth of their interdependence—their relationship—but they came to deny that in order to learn to control the elements," I said quietly. "Now our science is bringing us full circle and we are beginning to see the extent to which we are connected and in relationship to the world around us. We know that energy can neither be created nor destroyed, but that it constantly recycles and changes form. The atoms we inhale and ingest were stones, trees, animals, and other people only a short time before. A butterfly flapping its wings in the rainforest affects the weather on the other side of the planet. We are slowly coming to know the truth of our relatedness intellectually, but we do not yet carry this truth in our hearts."

"This is perhaps as it should be," the old man sighed. "You did not lose your sense of your place in a balanced world all at once. You will not recover it in an instant."

The old man added two more lines bisecting the circle at 45-degree angles. "So everything is alive, everything is conscious, everything is dynamic, and everything is connected." When he finished, he gestured at what he had drawn. "Now what do you have?"

"A web," I replied. "It looks like a spider's web."

"Yes," he nodded. "It is the Great Spider's web. We are all caught in this web, though we may pretend we are not. And, being caught in this web, what do you think happens when you move?"

I thought about this for a moment. I closed my eyes and imagined myself walking on this delicate web. "Every step I take would send vibrations out to the rest of the web. Everyone else in the web would know my movements."

"And this is the Fifth Stone, that everything responds. The seen and the unseen respond to the way we move in the world." He laughed softly to himself. "The web is constantly adjusting itself to our presence, our words, our thoughts, our actions. We are the web and the web is us. If the world is not how we would like it to be, we should look to how we are dreaming it, how we are moving through it, what we are creating with our thoughts and our hands."

I nodded. I have heard myself repeating some variation of "you create your own reality." It is something of a New Age mantra. This, too, would be a hard lesson for people in my world. The power of intention is sometimes mocked by those who need their causes and effects to be described by current scientific models, but intention is also a scary thing for people who want to believe. If our intentions—our dreams—define our experience, then we must be vigilant and consistent in our dreaming. It is difficult to spiritually come awake in a culture of sleepwalkers. Most of us on a path of spirit struggle to walk that path and stay awake and aware of our dreaming, but the culture and our own conditioning draw us so seductively back to sleep.

The idea that everything in the universe responds to us is both empowering and frightening. Power has been so abused in our culture that we have come to reject it. We have raised being a victim from an unfortunate condition to a moral position. As I thought about it, a question occurred to me. "Doesn't the idea that everything responds bring us full circle from being created to being creators?"

"That is what the Fifth Stone teaches us, that we are all creators. We create by how we pray, how we express gratitude, how we dance and sing, how we walk our path, and how we dream. When someone comes to me in need of healing, I need to know their prayers and how those prayers have been given material form in the waking world. Only then can I seek spirit guidance for them."

This seemed wise to me and in keeping with what I knew from my own practice. Sometimes the simple act of giving form to a prayer or intention through artistic expression was enough to shift a client's energetic balance back toward wholeness.

I traced the lines on my own sand drawing, turning it into a web, slowly repeating what I remembered. "Everything is alive. Everything is conscious. Everything transforms. Everything is connected. Everything responds."

"Aho," the old man added. I knew he was affirming what I was saying, acknowledging the truth in it using the Native American equivalent of Amen. I also knew I would be called back soon. The drumming CD was timed to last 30 minutes before providing a rapid callback rhythm, and I usually had a good sense of when the callback was about to occur.

"Grandfather," I began respectfully, "you are a spirit in my time and I am a spirit in yours. I will carry your words in my heart and share them with my people."

"Grandmother Spider's medicine is powerful. The Five Stones set us on the path of balance and beauty. How far any of us travel down that path is up to us. For some of us it is enough to carry the medicine in our own hearts and serve spirit. Others will hear the call to share their medicine dreams and serve the tribe. Still others will find themselves serving spirit and community, but will be called further to serve the healing needs of individuals. So share the Five Stones with your people. Grandmother Spider is not dead in your time, she is merely forgotten."

I became aware of the rapid beat of the callback rhythm somewhere far off. I knew that at any moment I would take to the air and return to my body somewhere in the night sky. "Grandfather, thank you for sharing your medicine with me. If I need your counsel, may I return to your fire?"

"I am an old man," he answered. "I do not know how many fires I have left. But if you have need of me, you are always welcome at my fire."

"How may I ask for you?"

"I am called, in your language, Gray Morning Bear. My mother's people are River Stone clan. My father is Badger clan."

"And I am called Tomas." I offered the name as my South and Central American teachers pronounce it.

"And you carry the medicine of two bears," he added. This surprised me, in that I had never been told that in the waking or the dreaming worlds, but at the same time it resonated deeply with a vision quest experience I had had in the mountains of Virginia. I felt that while I did not fully know what it meant, it was true. I also knew it was a kind of parting gift.

I stood and felt myself shift seamlessly back into the body of a hawk. I lifted myself up into the night sky. It seemed to take only seconds before I was high over the Earth. I found my dreaming body and slipped back inside it. I came awake slowly, remembering what I had seen and heard and felt. After a few minutes I drew my journal from my carry-on bag and sketched the symbols I had seen. I wrote down the principles I had heard about and made more notes to myself. After I was certain that I had recorded what I needed to remember, I closed the journal and let my mind play with the experience of the journey. I knew I had received a great gift. The Five Stones of Grandmother Spider's wisdom path were the guiding truths I had been looking for. They stated in the simplest of terms the core beliefs of a shamanic reality. They were as true for a shaman in the rain forest of the Amazon as they were for a Siberian shaman. They applied equally well to traditional and contemporary societies. They did not conflict with any wisdom teachings or cosmologies I had encountered.

I was also struck by Gray Morning Bear's description of the three-fold path. I had always been taught that a shaman serves spirit, community, and the individual, in that order. Piers Vitebsky's quote about shamanic cultures returned to me. The idea that many people might be shamans to a greater or lesser degree depending on their insight into the unseen world and its guiding principles seemed in perfect alignment with what I had just learned. Holding the wisdom of the Five Stones in our hearts would set us on the spirit path and encourage us to serve the unseen world, each in our own way. Serving spirit personally and privately—aligning ourselves with a different worldview—might be the way to return to balance. If some people then felt compelled to carry that teaching into community service, the work of rebalancing our world would be accelerated. Choosing to act as a healer for individuals would then be the third step on a spirit path that was shamanic.

All of this fit with the problem I had been wrestling with. But I knew that for me, the work was just beginning. I knew that in order to truly share Gray Morning Bear's wisdom, I would have to make a case for each of the Five Stones in language that resonated with people living urban contemporary lives. I would need to do more than just describe the Stones. I would need to find ways for people to come to experience the truth of each of the basic principles for themselves. Shamanism is not really an "ism" at all. Though I fall into the habit of referring to it as such, there is no doctrine, no sacred text; it is not a religion. It is an experiential path to spirit. For me to merely write about it would be like describing the shadow a thing casts rather than describing the thing.

Though I did not make this connection immediately, I would come to understand that embracing the five principles would lead quite naturally to five states of being, five kinds of action, five essential questions, and five fundamental practices for a personal expression of this ancient spiritual tradition.

The five fundamental practices include vision-shifting, journeying, shape-shifting, ceremony, and artistic expression. Because this is an experiential path, I'm going to ask you to take a first step down that path. In the following chapters I will be describing the fundamental practices as they relate to the principles. I would encourage you to experience the practices as you encounter them. They are in themselves simple acts, but their impact can be profound.

When I was an art student, one of the artists I most admired was a German by the name of Joseph Beuys. Beuys had been a very young pilot in the last days of World War II. His plane crashed in a remote area of the Crimea in the U.S.S.R. and he was found nearly frozen by a tribe of Tartars. They wrapped his body in animal fat and felt, insulating him in the only way they knew how, and he survived. He experienced in a very real way the classic shamanic near-death initiation. He went on to become an artist well known for his experimental and shamanic sculptures utilizing fat, felt, honey, fur, gold, and found objects. His work was sometimes obscure and seemed to refer to an inner world more than an outer one. His pieces were always about transformation. One of the quotes for which he is best known was "Everyone is an artist." This statement was provocative in the '60s, as it seemed to call into question the elevated status of artists. I think it is clear now that he was not saying that everyone is an Artist with a capital A, but that everyone needed to find a way to live and express himself or herself as an artist.

I think of this now because as we move more deeply into the Five Stones, the five principles of a shamanic worldview, that is what I am offering—the possibility that everyone is a shaman. Though there are communities that will find such a statement as preposterous and provocative as the art community found Beuys's proclamation in the '60s, I am not advocating that everyone become a Shaman with a capital S any more than Beuys was suggesting that we all become Artists. But the more we live by the principles of a shamanic worldview, the closer we return to the path of beauty and balance.

CHAPTER 2

Primal Alignment: Living in the Shaman's World

Shamans are personalities who live in a
deepened relationship to their cosmology.

John Grim,
The Shaman: Patterns of Religious Healing
among the Ojibway Indians

A COSMOLOGY IS A STORY THAT TELLS US where we came from and, more importantly, how we are to live. I would like to be able to say that I fully understood the cosmology of the Five Stones when they were first revealed to me, but that's not the case. They seemed reasonable, but I knew that in order to live them, I would need to challenge them and test their strength. More than just accepting the principles on faith, I had to do the "shamanic" thing and experience them in practice. I was, after all, engaged in a rather odd pursuit. I was looking for a way to align contemporary life more closely with the values of Stone Age, hunter-gatherer ancestors. I had no books I could consult. My Stone Age shaman ancestors left none behind. I could deduce ways of being from the anthropological research of primary hunter-gatherer cultures, but I had no way of testing the validity of these principles other than to live them as best I could. For this primal alignment I was seeking, I needed to try the five principles in a variety of situations and see how they applied. I needed to move into a deepened relationship with them.

Before I began to teach shamanic practice to students, I saw clients as a shamanic counselor. I had wonderful successes with both physical and emotional symptoms. One of the things I most liked about working through spirit and allowing spirit to work through me was that it was fast. I didn't need 30, 20, or even 10 sessions to begin to make progress. A first or second session, sometimes a third, was all that was needed to correct an imbalance. Most clients reported feeling much better, and most of the time their symptoms did not return. But in some respects I was blinded by the apparent effectiveness of shamanic intervention. Through spirit guidance I could correct a minor imbalance, remove a harmful force or entity, and sometimes break apart a negative pattern of belief. But without a more fundamental shift in the way that client was living his or her life, some new symptom would almost always return. Just like a Western medical doctor, I was dealing with the symptoms.

I was treating a woman for the spiritual and emotional malaise that plagues a lot of people. She wasn't exactly sick, but in some deep way she knew she would be if she couldn't give voice to her needs. She suffered from what in shamanic language is called soul loss. Soul loss is traditionally characterized by symptoms of depression, low energy, inability to deal with change, hopelessness, listlessness, and a sense of disinterest in life. It can manifest as frequent colds, flus, and other illnesses, immune deficiency diseases, chronic fatigue problems, and prolonged healing from minor complaints. As mentioned earlier, soul loss can occur from fear and trauma (soul fright), near-death experience (soul flight), long-term exposure to an imbalanced energetic relationship (soul theft), and a long period of ignoring the message and voice of your own soul (soul wandering). My diagnosis was soul wandering. We worked together for several sessions and she was pleased with the results, but I knew that all the "things" I knew how to do were not going to meet her needs. I explained this, feeling as if I had failed, but she was already a step ahead of me. "I know," she agreed. "What I'd like is for you to teach me."

When I think about this now, it makes such sense. What she knew intuitively was that she didn't need anything done *to* her. She needed to change how she was living to move more into alignment with spirit. I thought about this for a long time. I sought guidance from spirit in all the ways I knew how, and I was gifted with the vision of the Five Stones.

Anthropologist Hugh Brody writes in *The Other Side of Eden: Hunters, Farmers, and the Shaping of the World,* "The simple truth about a difficult decision is that its difficulty comes from the irresolvable quality of knowledge. A deep dilemma arises from the way in which accumulation of facts seems not to decide the issue. So what should be done? In the end, there is a need for some other kind of knowledge, some leap of imagination, some way of processing the facts so that they yield a conclusion. This is what dreams can do."

My dream, in the form of a shamanic journey, was the leap of imagination I needed, but still it took me a year to finally come to terms with how I might teach what I'd learned, and even more time to fully integrate the principles into my life and work.

So, just how goofy, radical, misguided, foolish (or substitute your own descriptive word) is the world when viewed from a shamanic perspective? Does the idea that the world is alive, conscious, dynamic, connected, and responsive really make sense for someone raised in an urban contemporary environment?

There seem to be two tests we might apply to the Five Stones and their principles. The first is the test of how closely these principles describe the world in which we live. Are they in alignment with how we currently perceive the world? The second test is to sidestep whether they are true or not and ask how our lives might be different if we acted as if they were true.

To see how this kind of test might apply to the Five Stones, let's pick one of the most difficult ideas for most people to grasp—that everything is alive.

If we rely on a biological definition of life, such as "The property or quality that distinguishes living organisms from dead organisms and inanimate matter, manifested in functions such as metabolism, growth, reproduction, and response to stimuli or adaptation to the environment originating from within the organism" (*American Heritage College Dictionary, Third Edition*), we might be hard pressed to find evidence that everything is alive.

But this definition begins to break down at the atomic level. Itzhak Bentov writes in *Stalking the Wild Pendulum: On the Mechanics of Consciousness,* "Suppose we stimulate an atom by applying ultraviolet light or other electromagnetic radiation to it. One or more of the electrons may get excited and respond by jumping into a higher orbit farther away from the nucleus. When we remove the stimulus, these electrons may drop back into their previous orbits and emit photons of a certain frequency in the process. By applying different stimuli, we shall elicit different responses from this system." The more complex a system is, the more possible responses it will have to a given stimulus. If an atom is a living thing because it can respond to stimuli and we are made up of atoms, shouldn't it be possible to see all things made up of atoms as having life in some form? Our Stone Age ancestors certainly thought so. They lived in an animist universe in which everything was animated by life force or spirit.

We acknowledge and respect life hierarchically. We may be willing to grant that all people, animals, and plants are alive, though the value we attribute to those lives varies greatly. We have a more difficult time accepting that other things, such as minerals or the products made from minerals, have the quality of life. But, again, if we move to the subatomic level, this distinction seems less and less relevant. At the quantum level, everything is made up of the same elements. The quantum particles that make up the simplest stone and the most complex machine are constantly being interchanged with the particles of plants, animals, and people. We breathe them in and out. We ingest and excrete them. They slide back and forth through the porous barrier of our skin.

We must also remember that the distinction between living organisms and inanimate matter is our own invention, and a rather recent one at that. So recent, in fact, that we haven't totally accepted it. We may not acknowledge that we consider things to have a life of their own, but we do act as if that were so. We still talk to our cars, our computers, and our machines as if they were living beings capable of responding to our urgings. We still curse the object we bang into as if it had set out to hurt us. The idea that the world and all the things in it are alive is how we perceive the world when we are not "thinking."

Our subtle senses, our primary senses, tell us that things do have living spirits. Perhaps this explains our desire to own and possess things. Acquiring things is actually just a way of acquiring their power, their spirit, their medicine. Advertisers know this. They sell us things by suggesting that we will acquire the power, magic, or style of those things if we own them. We don't need the speed and handling of a high-end sports car or the ruggedness of an off-road vehicle, but they do make us feel powerful, as if we can take on some of the spirit of the machine.

Rather than argue that this notion is foolish and emotional—some superstitious remnant of our past—the shaman would acknowledge that the car really does have a spirit, just as we perceive it to. What he might remind us, however, is that the spirit and the power within objects is something with which we can align ourselves, but it is never something we possess or own.

Again and again I see clients who have acquired all the symbols of wealth and power our culture respects, and still they are unhappy. Sometimes they're burdened by the very things they have acquired. Ask yourself if you really have time to clean, care for, maintain, use, appreciate, or honor all the things in your life. Be sure to include the machines and equipment, the tools and utensils, and all the art objects in your life in this inventory. Do you hire others to take care of your things? Do you own your things or do they own you? Do you sometimes feel overwhelmed by what you have? Do you feel that your possessions are calling to you to be used and handled? Do you feel guilty when you don't have the time to use or care for your things?

I'm not advocating that we shouldn't own things. Rather I want to point out that our things can sometimes have the same influence over us as other "living" organisms. In other words, the idea that the universe is alive does match how we currently perceive the world, at least at a subtle, emotional level. Our "things" are alive.

Our second test was how would our lives be different if we more fully or openly acted as if this principle were true. The first shamanic people were hunters and gatherers. They needed to observe and pay attention to everything; their very survival depended on it. They directed this level of attention not only toward the plants and animals in their world, but also to the stones, elements, and geographical features. They became excellent observers. They were vigilant. They developed techniques that allowed them to refine their ability to focus, to see at great distances, to distinguish sounds and smells, and to see patterns and hear messages expressed in the natural phenomena around them.

If everything is alive, I'm compelled to be aware of it, to give it my attention. It might seem overwhelming to need to pay attention to everything, but in reality, paying attention to everything is more about releasing than about doing. A shaman would strive to notice everything and then try to forget it. A shaman looks for what stands out. Snow in a dream of an Inuit hunter in the Arctic calls less attention to itself than snow in a dream of the tropics. A phrase or image that evokes a peculiar bodily sensation is more likely to be significant. An event that recurs or forms a pattern is something to which I should attend.

So how would considering the world to be alive and paying attention to it change how we live? We might rediscover the wonder of a child's view. Every child knows that things are alive, and every encounter is potentially rich and magical. We have to learn to be bored. We might want to own fewer things, but to care for and respect the spirit of the things we own. We might want to judge what we surround ourselves with by the quality of the energy those things carry rather than what the culture at large thinks of those things. We might spend a little time each day caring for special objects. We might be more open to the voice of spirit manifesting through objects.

James Hillman writes in *The Soul's Code: In Search of Character and Calling,* "Since anything around can nourish our souls by feeding imagination, there is soul stuff out there. So why not admit, as does deep ecology, that the environment itself is ensouled, animated, inextricably meshed with us and not fundamentally separate from us?"

If we consider the world to be alive and deserving of our attention, we might learn to look and listen deeply before making assumptions. Most of us live in a world where we are so rushed that we listen and observe only enough to make a judgment and respond. We literally jump to conclusions. We listen to just enough of what a person is actually saying to think we understand. Once we "think we understand," we essentially shut down our capacity to listen and begin to formulate our response. Conversely, the ability to "listen from the heart" is one of the fundamental principles from which shamans operate.

This basic act of paying attention not only flows from my sense of the aliveness of the world around me, but it also helps me to be more inclusive and discriminating. I am inclusive because everything matters, and I am discriminating because I choose to focus my attention on what stands out, what recurs, what forms a pattern.

We can apply these two tests to each of the Five Stones and find ways in which the Stones not only accurately describe the world as we experience it but also improve our relationship to that world. Shamanism is, if nothing else, a very practical spiritual path. A shaman or a shamanic practitioner doesn't need to believe in anything. He or she knows from direct observation and experience.

So what does it really mean to say that the universe is living, conscious, dynamic, connected, and responsive? What I discovered as I worked with these simple guiding principles is that if you accept them, they lead quite naturally into states of what I will call primal alignment. From these states of being flow a series of primary shamanic practices that dramatically affect how we live.

This revelation was exciting. As I worked with the Five Stones, I began to feel as if I understood how the tools of the classic shaman came to be developed. Dreamwork, energetic sensitivity, trance journeying, shape-shifting, ritual, prayer, and the sacred arts all made perfect sense as they flowed from the fundamental principles of the Five Stones. It was almost like I was moving back in time to retrieve the wisdom of my Stone Age ancestors— becoming a dream archeologist.

PRINCIPLE #1:
The First Stone
Everything is alive.

The principle that everything is alive suggests that everything is worth my attention. We are thrust into a state of primal fascination. We learn to be vigilant and observant and see things as they are. This state prompts us to study and to analyze—to see what something is and how it is distinctive without judging or making assumptions. As we engage the world this way, we find that our consciousness begins to change and we shift our way of seeing. This shamanic way of seeing is the practice I call "vision-shifting." When we vision-shift, we see patterns that were otherwise hidden.

We take into account the unseen, unspoken influences in a situation. We develop a kind of second attention and learn to read the double signals that come from secondary processes such as dreams, visions, intuitive flashes, synchronous events, and so on. Vision-shifting increases the range of our vision. It is similar to what trackers refer to as peripheral field vision. It means taking in the whole rather than walking as if in a tunnel, with a tight, narrow focus on what's ahead. When we begin to see energetically, we have a feel for the essential nature of things. We begin to see things as the movement of energies within dynamic fields of energy.

When we encounter signs in the waking world or dream images in the dreaming world, we learn to observe before doing anything else. We ask ourselves what we are actually perceiving. What is the nature of the object, the animal, the person, or the event that has shown up in our life? How is it distinctive from other similar events? What do we *know* to be true about it, versus what we *assume* to be true?

This practice of observing first is not just a spiritual discipline; it can also have an important impact on day-to-day living. When we don't make assumptions in our conversations with others, we tend to hear more of what is actually being said. We try to withhold our opinions and attitudes about a thing before we have engaged in the disciplined practice of seeing what is actually before us or listening to what is actually being said.

The native people of North America have a practice known as council. Sitting in a council circle is fundamentally about listening and paying attention in a profound way. Often a talking stick or talking feather is passed from person to person to signify who has the right to speak. When someone else holds the talking stick, we are expected to listen to what is said with compassion and an open heart. The key is to really listen. We should not be planning a rebuttal for the future or cogitating on what was said two speakers in the past. We also should not take up the talking stick simply to hear our own voice. We should not hold back from speaking, but we should say only what needs to be said, what hasn't already been given voice to.

Listening from the heart and giving someone our complete attention is a difficult thing to do for extended periods of time, so when we have someone's full attention we should use that gift respectfully. It is not enough that we speak the truth in situations like this. We must learn to distill the truth down to an essence that needs to be shared.

When we are in primal alignment with the first principle, we will be observant and attentive to the living universe around us.

PRINCIPLE #2:
The Second Stone
Everything is conscious.

From the idea that everything has its own form of conscious awareness, we learn to be present. If things can be conscious, they can have their own needs and desires. Learning about those needs and desires can tell us a lot about why they are in our lives. If things can have consciousness, we can learn to enter into true dialogue with them. We can learn what the unseen forces around us want by attending to the conscious forms they take.

In a dream, we might ask what a book wants or what a stained glass window wants. A book as conscious object may want to be read, to be opened, to be remembered, or to be referred to—all things that might fulfill the higher purpose, the soul purpose, of a book. A stained glass window might want to transform the color of light, to alter the energy of a space, or to tell a story with pictures.

In waking life, we can ask what those around us want. We can ask what wants to happen in any situation. We can consider what is trying to be born or to manifest.

By considering the consciousness of what surrounds us and what we encounter, we learn about the power of acknowledgement. If you've ever felt that what you most needed was not for anything to be done about your problem or situation but for someone to simply acknowledge it, you understand the gift you bring when you acknowledge someone else. What the shaman knows is that acknowledging the consciousness of the unseen forces around you is as important as acknowledging the feelings of the people around you.

The dictionary defines consciousness as "Having an awareness of one's environment, and one's own existence, sensations, and thoughts." The problem here is that self-awareness is a tricky thing to evaluate. We might easily say that stones and bricks are not self-aware, but what about plants and trees? When subjected to stress, plants display very different electromagnetic signatures. When I am asleep and dreaming, I feel self-aware even though I appear to be unconscious. Perhaps consciousness or, more precisely, our perception of consciousness, requires a certain attunement. There are radio waves all around us, interpenetrating us, but we can't hear them without a special receptor, and even that receptor needs to be tuned to the right frequency for a particular broadcast wave.

One might define a shaman as a person with the ability to adjust his or her receptor to the right frequency for a particular expression of consciousness. Shamans do this frequency modulation with the help of consciousness-altering practices, but we all experience a form of this frequency modulation in our dreams. With practice, a dreamer can choose to dream about specific issues or even become lucid or awake in her dream.

The practice of shamanic frequency modulation or consciousness altering that gives us more control over our ability to engage in dialogue with a conscious world is the deliberate altering of consciousness. Shamans are masters of this state, but all members of primal social groups would have had access to the experience of altered consciousness.

PRINCIPLE #3:
The Third Stone
Everything is dynamic.

If we embrace and understand that it is the nature of living things to move, change, and transform, then we are compelled to develop flexibility. When we are in primal alignment with the third principle, we become surfers rather than wasting our energy trying to hold back the wave of change that is coming. The attentiveness we developed coming into primal alignment with the first principle—that everything is alive—helped us to become sensitive to energy and the energetics of a situation. Through that primal alignment we develop a sense of when energy is moving, which way it is flowing, and when or where it is blocked. By coming into primal alignment with the second principle—that everything is conscious—we learn that we can engage in dialogue with people, animals, objects, and even elemental forces. Now we extend that by asking the moving energies what they want, where they want to move to, and how they would like to move. Finally, we learn to move energies not by mastering them but by merging with them. This is the shamanic practice of shape-shifting.

Shape-shifting is a profoundly different way of engaging the world. Our Stone Age ancestors were shape-shifters. They didn't fail to hold back flooding rivers with dams because they weren't smart enough to do so or because they simply lacked the technology, but because it would not have occurred to them to place themselves in opposition to the natural movement of the river. They considered the river to be a living, conscious entity with its own desires. There is a wonderful illustration of this in the film *Out of Africa*, the story of Karen Blixen's life in colonial Africa. She is giving instructions to one of her servants to dam a stream to create a pond on her property. Her servant seems a little perplexed at this idea and argues that "This water must go home to Mombassa." When she answers that the water can go home after they have made a pond, he tries once again to express himself, "But this water *lives* in Mombassa."

Shape-shifting as we commonly think of it involves taking on an animal form. Our Stone Age hunter-gatherer ancestors shape-shifted into the forms of their prey to better understand how to hunt them. Sometimes they shape-shifted into the forms of powerful hunting animals to learn different ways to hunt. At still other times they shape-shifted into animals that had a profound relationship with an elemental force such as wind, rain, or snow to better understand or even subtly influence the weather.

The hunter-gatherer ethos of our Stone Age ancestors was one of adapting to change—influencing events by merging with the forces, understanding them, and applying the minimal amount of pressure at the precise tipping point. In the modern world we have replaced this idea with the notion that we can control our surroundings by force or by standing in direct opposition to them. But just underneath the surface we can see signs of shape-shifting all around us. Rather than fight the reality of changing tastes, some of our most enduring celebrities have shape-shifted.

The idea of reinventing oneself, of taking on a new skin, has helped performers as different as Bob Dylan and Madonna remain not only popular but also vital. We shape-shift when we match our patterns of speech and behavior to those around us. We shape-shift when we try to "get inside" the mind of a client to close a sale or a deal. We shape-shift when we become the person those around us want us to be, and sometimes we run the same risks as shamanic shape-shifters—encountering difficulty in finding and returning to our true form.

The practice of shape-shifting involves a willingness to sense the wave moving beneath us and to respond by adjusting our balance at ever-deepening levels of awareness.

PRINCIPLE #4:
The Fourth Stone
Everything is connected.

Once we accept that everything exists in relationship to everything else, we learn to be respectful. Building on what we have learned, we understand that once we have studied a thing and understood its essence, once we have acknowledged its needs and desires and merged with it to understand how it moves and where it is going, we can choose to form an alliance with it in sacred reciprocity. This is what the shamanic practice of ritual and ceremony is designed to accomplish. When we are in primal alignment with the fourth principle, we use ritual to form alliances with both the seen and unseen forces and to restore balance and harmony by honoring those relationships.

Ritual and ceremony are where our spiritual work takes physical form. We connect ourselves to the patterns and the web of life through ceremony. We give the sacred patterns visible form through the creation of altars, offerings, and vessels for spirit to inhabit.

While the rituals of communal spirituality might have devolved into the passive experience we participate in by attending the theater or the sterile, repetitive habits of action found in many religious services, we still practice or are capable of being moved by ritual. A psychologist might tell us that a ritual makes us feel good because it connects us to other people. A doctor might admit that a ritual can help us clarify an intention to heal in such a way as to improve our state of mind and, hence, our immune system. Our Stone Age ancestors would probably see it differently.

They would have thought it obvious to even the most casual observer that we are part of an interconnected web of exchanges. It is not such a stretch to imagine that there are practices that allow us to more fully participate in that web. These protocols of reciprocity and relationship are the foundation of ritual. If we ask for help without being willing to help in return, we break the bonds of a relationship. If we take what is offered to us without an expression of gratitude, we further erode the bonds of a relationship. If we fail to acknowledge the nature of our relationships and our interconnectedness, we isolate ourselves and place ourselves in opposition to the way the world seems to want to work.

PRINCIPLE #5:

The Fifth Stone

Everything is responsive.

The universe responds to our most sacred intentions. This principle is not as simplistic as it is sometimes interpreted to be. No, we do not always get the things we think we want, especially within the time frame we think is appropriate. This is especially true when we are focused on the acquisition of material things. On the other hand, I have seen far too many examples of prayers being answered in spiritual, emotional, and even material form to dismiss the power of intention. The critical factor, or primal alignment, with the fifth principle seems to be that we take responsibility for being creators and learn to act creatively while honoring the two C's: compassion and clarity. When we set an intention that comes from the heart—from a place of compassion— it has more energy behind it. When we are clear about what we are praying for and about our intentions—when we know the "why" as well as the "what"—the universe's response is often more in alignment with what we asked for.

When we understand that the universe actually responds to our actions, it leads us to two conclusions. The first is that the life we have is the universe's response to our prayers and intentions. If we have not been conscious of praying or of setting intentions, we must remember that to the conscious universe, much of what we say or do may seem prayerlike. How we choose to live our lives may be the equivalent of setting an intention. This is where the idea of clarity comes in. Can we learn to be clear about what we are asking for, whether we are asking consciously or unconsciously? I have counseled people who have lived in unhappy relationships, too paralyzed to do anything but wish for something better, and who have then been shocked when their spouses requested a divorce. Clarity also relates to the idea that before we arrive at this fifth principle, before we utilize the power of intention, we have used other tools and practices to align ourselves with our soul's purpose. We have studied the situation in which we find our- selves, separating facts and the things we have real evidence of from our assumptions and opinions. Then we have acknowledged the needs of the other, questioning not just what we want, but what is wanted from us. We have developed a feel for which way the energy wants to move and become clear about whether we are setting ourselves in opposition to it or are learning to move with it. Finally, we have become clear as to how we are connected to what we want and the relationships that will be affected if we get what we want. So, when we set an intention from this place of clarity, we are less likely to sabotage our own prayers by allowing fear to interfere with putting the appropriate energy behind them.

The second conclusion we reach is that we are co-creators. Shamans are not mystics or passive visionaries; they engage the world with creative action. They perform, sing, dance, enact, tell stories, paint pictures, and create beautiful tools and objects. We, too, can learn to engage in the sacred creative cycle that is the source of what we call art, but which encompasses much more than what art is commonly perceived to be. We can change our physical world to reflect a change in the spirit world or to ask for a change in the spirit world. We can learn to bridge waking and dreaming with creative action and intention.

Recording Your Journey

One of the first things I will ask you to do is to get a journal to record your experiences on this path to Stone Age wisdom. Earlier I mentioned that I felt as if I was moving backward in time to recover the sources of shamanic practice and to seek out the wisdom of my hunter-gatherer ancestors. As you embark on this path, you, too, will be working as a kind of dream archeologist. Some of the things that will happen to you will defy your expectations. You will be shocked and amazed at what you can learn once you open up to a new level of reality. Because these experiences will seem so incredible, it is important that you document them.

Keeping a journal devoted to your experiences dreaming, vision-shifting, journeying, shape-shifting, bringing ceremony into your life, and acting creatively will give you confirmation and support. Your journal will also become your best resource for the hidden significance of various dream- and waking-world imagery and experiences. Remember that primal alignment with the first principle requires that you learn to slow down and study. Your journal is your textbook for studying. In it you will record your encounters with the unseen world and map the energetic world that unfolds before you. You will plan simple ceremonies and do personal inventories to become clear about your intentions.

Before we explore the shamanic practices that flow from being in primal alignment with the Five Stones, I think it would be worthwhile to consider dreams and dreamwork. For the shaman, as undoubtedly for our Stone Age ancestors, dreams are as important as anything that happens while waking. Learning to attend to dreams falls under the heading of vision-shifting, while utilizing the full capability of dream states falls more appropriately under the heading of journeying. I have elected to separate dreamwork out and give it a chapter of its own for two reasons. First, it is one of the most accessible forms of guidance from and interaction with the unseen world. We all dream, and every dream can tell us something about the state of our soul. So I set it aside to emphasize it. The second reason is that shamanic dreamwork, flowing as it does from the five principles, provides a beautiful working example of how the principles weave together in our lives.

CHAPTER 3

Living by Dreams:
Contemporary
Shamanic Dreamwork

*If I have any therapeutic intention it is to help the bear,
to understand it and bring its obscure intentions across
from the dream world into the daily world we all share.*

James Hillman,
Dream Animals

FOR THE SHAMAN, AS FOR HER STONE AGE ancestors, dreams are considered that time when the veil between the worlds is most permeable. It is in dreams that we experience the overlapping nature of the seen and unseen worlds most clearly. We can wake from a profound dream to find ourselves changed in some significant way. We can recall a dream as if it actually occurred in the waking world. The characters and the landscapes of our waking world often intrude on our dreaming consciousness.

Perhaps the most important reason for attending to your dreams is that they can show you the ways in which you are out of balance in your relationship with your soul's mission. Dreams can help you understand the misalignment between your primary and secondary perceptions and expressions. Sometimes these dreams come in forms that are so clear and direct that they need no further examination. Other times, the feelings elicited in the dream will be enough to cause an energetic shift. Most of the time, however, dreams need to be unfolded and more fully experienced to reveal themselves. The shaman would say that dreams are only ours in the sense that we experienced them and shared them. But we do not own the dream, the story of the dream, or the characters and objects within the dream. They have their own lives, consciousness, and capacity for communicating. Our job is to discover what our dreams want from us.

Shamanic dreamwork shares some elements with contemporary dreamwork traditions. Both are exploratory processes, both avoid projecting the opinions of the dreamworker onto the dreamer, and both are open-ended—meaning they avoid providing fixed meanings for specific imagery. But while contemporary dreamwork therapists such as Arnold Mindell, James Hillman, Robbie Bosnak, and Sven Doehner have pioneered a kind of dreamwork much more closely aligned with shamanic tradition, shamanic dreamwork differs from dreamwork that emerges from a psychological tradition in several key ways.

The shamanic tradition of dreamwork is based on the idea that there is a seen and an unseen world, and that the unseen world is the template according to which the seen world manifests. The unseen world is no less real for being unseen. A dream's landscapes, objects, and characters have lives of their own. To quote from James Hillman's *Dream Animals* his comments about a woman dreaming about a polar bear,

I take all dreams as belonging first of all to the figures in them, mainly to the bear in this instance. Although a dream is said to "belong" to the dreamer, inasmuch as she "had" it and wrote it down, I doubt that the bear is "hers." Rather, I like to pretend that the bear is the occasion for the dream and even for transmitting the dream from her to me and from me to you. I conceive myself to be a catalyst communicator, connecting the animal to the human world, to, let's say, in these dreams of polar bears, their agent.

The shamanic view is to honor the spirit of the thing that is trying to communicate with us through the dream. It is not merely a symbol or something to be understood, but a presence to be attended to and a consciousness with its own desires. We owe our first allegiance not to what the dreamer wants but to what the dream wants.

In the psychotherapeutic tradition of dreamwork, the therapist does not interpret a dream or say what the dream means, but rather encourages the client to explore multiple meanings of the dream. This distance helps keep the therapist from robbing the patient of his or her power and encourages the patient to own the message of the dream. But in traditional shamanic communities, consulting a shaman to interpret a dream is not a therapeutic relationship. Dreams are used for diagnosing and curing. If I ask a shaman what my dream means, I'm not likely to get the response, "Well, what do *you* think it means?"

The shaman or shamanic counselor may use dreams or dream information for diagnosis or healing in the following ways.

Proxy dreaming. This is when the shaman has a precognitive dream for a client in advance of working with that client. It can also occur after seeing a client, when the intention is set to get healing wisdom about a particular client from a dream.

Dream navigation. This is when a shaman uses a trance or a dream incubation technique to reenter a client's dreamscape. This is sometimes done to gather more information, but can also be used to effect changes in the dream story and therefore in the waking reality that manifests from the dream.

Interpretation/storytelling. Sometimes, the shaman may guide the client in reexperiencing and retelling the dream while reading/listening to/observing the client energetically. In this process, the shaman may focus on key archetypal questions, such as the ones that flow from the Five Stones. The shaman may also interpret or retell the dream as a mythic, archetypal, or energetic story.

Creative engagement. The shaman may guide the client to respond to the dream at a primal, imagistic, or physical level. The client may be encouraged to move into the dream to act out or embrace the experience, track a body sensation, or make a sound. He or she may be directed to make something or find something to bridge waking and dreaming. The client may be given a task or quest based on a dream. Sometimes the shaman creates something from a dream image.

Ceremony. The shaman may engage the community in group dreaming on behalf of the client. This is generally not an intellectual process where everyone seeks to explain the dream, but rather a harvesting of additional imagery.

What matters most for our purposes is to find a productive way of unfolding the imagery of our dreams and receiving the guidance those dreams offer us. For that reason, we will focus on the interpretive aspect of shamanic dreamwork. Remember that what we want to develop in ourselves is the ability to study and acknowledge the energy or the archetypal nature of the dream. We want to be aware of the highly personal imagery of the dream and at the same time pull back from it—to see the energetic pattern of the story beneath the surface. We want to know what the dream wants of us. This is doubly important because the awareness we bring to our dream life and its imagery is the same kind of attention we want to direct at our waking life. This vision-shifted way of seeing is what helps us perceive the fields and the movement of energies.

I have had a lifelong relationship with my dream imagery. I have studied dreamwork with Henry Reed, David Gordon, and Sven Doehner, and I have learned much from their methods, but I have also sought out what information I could find about how traditional shamans and healers use dreams. My own method evolved from my experience with my teachers and my own understanding of the Five Stones. Each of the five principles connected to the Five Stones suggests some key questions that help unfold the imagery of the dream and reveal the energetic template or story beneath.

To access the guidance of the unseen world as it manifests itself in your dreams, you need to be able to remember your dreams, unfold the imagery of a dream, and bridge the waking and dreaming worlds.

Remembering Your Dreams

Everyone dreams. You may not remember your dreams, but you do dream. If you don't remember your dreams, there are some practical steps you can take to improve your ability to hold onto your dreams after you wake. But even if you do remember your dreams, it's a good idea to review some of the tips below. You never know when you might find yourself experiencing difficulty remembering dreams. Even committed dreamers can go through dry spells when they can't remember their dreams. If you have always remembered your dreams but never unfolded the imagery of a dream, you may be surprised by what you find. If you are exploring delicate or sensitive soul territory for the first time, this can sometimes lead to a backlash in your psyche that prevents you from remembering your dreams as your ego tries to defend itself.

Tips for Dream Recall

If you're having trouble recalling your dreams, try the following techniques to get you started.

Tell yourself that you will remember a dream. Setting an intention is the single most important thing you can do to improve your ability to remember a dream. As you fall asleep at night, instead of counting sheep, repeat to yourself as many times as you can that you will remember a dream in the morning. Keep your shaman's traveling journal and a pen (and maybe a flashlight) beside your bed and within easy reach.

When you first wake up, lie still for a while. The memory of a dream is keyed to the body posture we were in when we dreamed it. As you wake in the morning, try not to make any dramatic movements. If you catch yourself rolling over, simply roll back into your previous position and move to the next step.

Rehearse the dream several times before moving. Before stretching, rolling over, getting out of bed, or engaging in any other physical activities, rehearse the dream. Replay the dream in your mind and try to recall as much detail as possible. Follow the chain of events in the dream as far back as you can go. Repeat this process several times, as if recollecting the plot of a good movie, but be careful not to fall back asleep. Move to the next step only after you think you have as much material as you can remember.

Record the dream in words and pictures. Try to write your dreams out in the first-person present tense as a stream-of-consciousness narrative. This seems to reinforce the quality of being in the dream. It helps you relive it as you recall and record it. I also find it useful to add little pictures, maps, or diagrams to my text. Record the objective details of the dream. Write out as much as you remember, as far back as you remember. Story is important, but the imagery and details of the dream are even more important. Don't try to give meaning to anything as you write—just write. If you can only recall a single image, record that in as much detail as possible. After you have described the objective details of the dream, record how you felt upon waking. This is important because dreams will often read as nightmarish even though the feeling upon waking was not one of fright or anxiety. Be sure to record whether any emotions or experiences from the dream lingered.

If you still have difficulty remembering your dreams, try the following tips.

Vary your sleeping/waking schedule. Does the sound of an alarm jolt you awake? Try setting your intention to recall a dream over a weekend or a holiday, when you have the time to sleep late and wake slowly. Conversely, if you always sleep late and wake slowly, try setting an alarm for the early hours of the morning to see if you have better recall.

Make a habit out of it. Don't let yourself off the hook just because you don't recall any dreams. Write down the first things that come into your head. Write down whatever spontaneous images or thoughts occur to you. Sometimes this can trigger dream recall. It also sets a pattern that you will record something. It puts your psyche on notice that even if you don't like the discipline of writing, failure to remember a dream won't exempt you from the process.

Sometimes we lose our ability to remember dreams even when we normally have great recall. If the flow or pattern of your dreaming is interrupted, consider the following possibilities:

Your ego may be challenged by the messages of the dream. Sometimes our dreams suggest life changes that seem too radical, too uncomfortable, or too difficult. If we tend to establish rules and limits about how much change we are willing to accept, we can experience a shutdown of dream imagery. On the other hand, the same tendency might produce dramatic and frightening nightmares as Spirit uses our soul's worst fears to get through to us.

You may not have honored or acted on the guidance of your dreams in the past. Imagine a friend who is always asking you for help. You give the best advice every time you are asked, but your friend never takes that advice. How patient and persistent are you willing to be before you begin to feel as if your advice is not valued? If we continually receive dream guidance from spirit upon which we fail to act, the well of guidance, in effect, runs dry. You do not need to act on every dream, but spirit likes to be honored. It likes to be fed through ritual. Paint your dream or find an object to represent it on your personal altar. Make a nature offering in gratitude for the dream's guidance, even if you are unable at the time to follow it.

You may be caught in a field of strong emotions. Trauma, worry, grief, anger, fear, or even intense love and erotic passion can temporarily interfere with our receiving dream guidance. It's almost as if we need the respite more than we need the guidance.

Your sleep cycle might have been disturbed. Illness, drug use, change of routine, the arrival of a new baby, or the arrival or departure of a new energy within a household can all disturb your dreaming life. Sometimes simple external alterations can temporarily interfere with dream recall.

Keep in mind that the situations mentioned above, in certain people, may be just as likely to produce an excess of dreams or a plethora of highly memorable dreams as they are to cause dream recall to be interrupted. Whatever the cause, the link to spirit guidance through dreams can still be rebuilt by returning to the steps in "Tips for Dream Recall," on page 73.

✦ STONE AGE WISDOM PRACTICE #2:
Unfolding the Imagery of the Dream
Let's begin with a simple dream and look at how the principles underlying the Five Stones produce questions that can help illuminate the energetic message of the dream. The best way to do this is with a partner to ask you the questions and go through the retelling part, but you can do it on your own if you avoid the temptation to bypass certain steps.

A man dreams he is in a department store. He has stopped on his way home from work to buy a gift for his wife. It is neither a birthday nor an anniversary, he simply wants to surprise her with a gift. He goes to the perfume counter, but the salesperson is a young woman with spiked black hair, body piercings, tattoos, and ripped punk clothing. He does not think this person will be able to help him pick out the right gift for his wife. In fact, the salesperson seems a little threatening. Despite her appearance, however, she really seems to want to help. She asks him about his wife and he describes his wife to the young woman. The salesperson compliments him on how well he knows his wife. She then begins to sample different perfumes for the man. He likes the smells of the perfume but does not think the packaging matches the kind of person his wife is. He is now aware of a crow or big black bird standing on the counter among the perfume bottles. The young woman senses the man's confusion and suddenly seems to have no patience for it. She grabs him by his tie and tells him there is nothing that would be right for his wife at her counter. Then she suggests that he try upstairs in the lingerie department. The man backs away and turns to take the escalator up to the lingerie department. Then he decides he does not want to go that way and tries to turn and walk down the "up" escalator. The crow flies at his face as if to keep him from getting off the escalator. He falls down and when he stands up he notices that his shoelace is caught in the escalator. He is struggling to free it and beginning to panic when he wakes up.

The dreamer reports that he wakes with an anxiety that comes not from being stuck, but from being forced to continue shopping on this new level. Notice that the dream is told in present tense and there is no attempt to explain things or provide background during the telling. This is important because what we are trying to avoid is the tendency to rush to an interpretation. We want to respect the imagery and the evidence of the dream first. The first thing the dreamer might tuck away in his mind is to be conscious of his shoelaces the next time he finds himself on an escalator or perhaps to watch any loose clothing the next time he finds himself around heavy automated machinery. This would be short-range psychic guidance. The mid- to long-range soul guidance comes with the unfolding of the dream. To unfold the dream, we need to consider two aspects of the dream: the dreamspirits and the dreamstory.

A dreamspirit is anything that shows up in a dream. It may be a person, an animal, a monster or alien, an object or substance, a place, a geographic feature, or a force of nature. It may look familiar or it may look strange. It may look like your mother, daughter, or boss, or a famous celebrity, but it isn't. It's a dreamspirit in the likeness of one of those people. Why it has chosen to appear in that form is what this process will unfold. Remember that in the shaman's world, everything is alive. The dreamworld is inhabited by dreamspirits.

The dreamstory is the relationship that is woven between the dreamspirits in the course of the dream. It is what happens in the dream. The actions of the dreamstory relate to actions in waking life the same way that the images of dreamspirits relate to people and objects in waking life; they are not the same. When you die in a dream, when you make love to someone, when you kill or injure someone or violate a taboo, it does not mean that you secretly want to do these things. These actions are chosen by the Spirit that is dreaming us because there is an energy that needs to be evoked. What that energy is and why it needs to be evoked now is what this process of shamanic dreamwork is designed to reveal.

First Stone Questions
(Everything Is Alive)

Where and when does the dream take place?

The first thing I would like to know is where the dream took place. This can tell me what field the issue of the dream is operating in. I will then reduce this to an energetic description. In this case, the location was a department store, so I asked, "What is a department store?" (Not how do you feel about department stores, but what are they in themselves?) The dreamer offered his sense that department stores are places for buying things, where money is exchanged for products, and I countered by asking how they are different from other places where you can buy things. He added that they are places where there are a lot of things to choose from. He also added that a department store is a big store in which a lot of little stores are organized into departments. We also noted that the timing of the dream is a liminal time. It is the in-between time as he transitions from his work world to his home world. From an energetic perspective, I suggested that the field of the dream (or the core issue of the dream as it relates to the man's life) is one of exchanges of energy being made in an environment where there are many choices and options. I further suggested that the dream imagery tells us that the field may involve the challenge of integrating or balancing two important worlds or aspects of life. I then proposed that we hold this as a possibility while we move on with the dream images. I don't expect that this first impression will always be complete or even right, just that we hold it as a possibility while we unfold the dreamspirits and the dreamstory. I do not try to relate the dream to specifics of the man's life.

What are the qualities of the people, objects,
or energies of the dream?

Since everything is alive, I have an obligation to pay attention to everything in my dream. One way of doing this is to ask the question, "What is it?" I could inquire about any or all of the dreamspirits (objects or characters), but I focus on some that stand out. What is perfume? The dreamer responded that it is a nice scent, that it is one of the subtle things that makes a woman attractive, that it is part of a woman's image. I suggested that the dream imagery might have to do with the dreamer's perception of his wife. There is a conflict in the dream between what smells good (a very physical, earthy response) and what seems appropriate according to a preconceived notion (a very mental, airy response).

I also asked what qualities the dreamspirit of the punk salesperson holds. The dreamer responded that she is rebellious, that she doesn't care what other people think, that she is edgy, risky, and a little dangerous. I suggested that we consider those qualities as being important in the process of making choices. Those qualities might be energies to which the dreamer has access. I asked about crows and the dreamer said that they are smart birds and that they are cunning and crafty about getting what they want. He laughed and added that witches have them as familiars. I decided to play with this a little and suggested that perhaps the crow is a messenger from the scarier side of feminine power.

We talked about escalators, and the dreamer said they are like stairs and elevators. He said that, like elevators, escalators take you up without your having to work, and that like stairs, you are always free to choose whether to climb faster or turn around and go back down. I asked whether in the dream he felt that he had that freedom, and he responded that the crow and the shoelace being stuck kept him from retreating. We talked about a few more things, then moved on to the second set of questions.

It is important to remember not to ignore the dreamspirits that show up as significant objects in the dream. It is tempting to focus on dreamspirits that take the form of people or animals and ignore objects, substances, or elemental forces, but in this case much would have been lost by not attending to perfume and escalators. On the other hand, unless one simply has unlimited time, it is not necessary to attend to every single object the dreamer can recall. Scan everything, then try to forget most of it. Trust what seems to move forward to you or hide from you in a dream. My friend Sven Doehner describes what he looks and listens for in a dreamspirit as that thing that "hooks" him.

Second Stone Questions
(Everything Is Conscious)

What do the characters or objects in the dream want?

Remember that though it may feel awkward at first, we are going to try to get inside or shape-shift into the dreamspirits. This requires a playful bit of personification and a willingness to constantly ask, "Do I have evidence of that in the dream?" Here are some of the things the dreamer suggested:

• The department store wants me to make a choice. If I leave the store without choosing something, the store will feel sad. Its soul purpose will not be fulfilled.

• The perfume wants to find the right woman to blend with. Perfume wants to support or participate in the image of a woman's attractiveness.

• The salesperson wants me to choose based on my senses, as opposed to my mental image. She wants me to rely on my more primal sense (smell), as opposed to my mental image of my wife (vision). She gets impatient when I can't or won't do this. The evidence of the dream also suggests that the salesperson really wants me to find something for my wife.

• The escalator wants me to move up effortlessly. Moving up suggests transcendence or growth.

• The crow that I've identified as a smart bird wants me to keep moving forward and not quit, turn back, or change my mind.

• The reason it's important to stick with the evidence of the dream is to keep assumptions about motivation within the dream itself. For instance, if the dreamer had said that the salesperson was a young punk with an attitude who didn't want to help him, I would have countered that that may have been a true experience he'd had with a punk salesperson in waking life, but it doesn't reflect the behavior of the dreamspirit in this dream.

What wants to happen in the dream?

This may seem like a different way of asking the previous question, but it tends to reveal a larger pattern. In this case, the dreamer summed it up nicely by expressing that the right gift wants to be given.

Third Stone Questions (Everything Moves)

Where are there examples of movement in the dream?

Remember the principle that healthy things move and transform. The presence of movement in a dream is an indicator of health and balance. Lack of movement indicates an imbalance. There is no judgment connected with either state. In this dream, the most significant examples of movement are the movement into the department store and the movement up in the escalator. The imagery of the dream suggests that moving into the place of choosing is what the soul wants and that persistence is required in moving forward.

Where are there examples of stuck energy
or a noticeable lack of movement?
What interferes with movement in the dream is the dreamer's inability to trust his senses in making a choice of perfumes. This keeps the dreamer stuck at the perfume counter so long that the salesperson literally scares him into leaving. The second instance of being stuck is the attempt to turn around on the escalator and reverse his movement. This leads to being caught on the escalator and truly stuck.

Is there a conflict that seems to emerge in the dream?
At this point the dreamer identified that the conflict has to do with his needing to make a choice based on his real feelings, and his inability to do so.

Now I can retell the dream from an energetic, almost mythic perspective. When doing this for others I use "he" or "I" to avoid projecting onto the dreamer and to acknowledge that this is one possibility. Even when I do it for myself, I find it is helpful to refer to myself in the third person.

A man is looking for a way to integrate or balance the energies of work and home, specifically as it impacts on his relationship with his wife. It is not an issue that he does not have an answer for. Rather, his problem is that he has too many possible choices and does not know how to choose. The unlikely ally he acquires (the punk salesperson) in this quest carries the energy of rebellion and risk and rejecting the status quo. The first possibility that presents itself has to do with shifting the image he has of his wife. He is asked to choose based on new or unfamiliar criteria. He is asked to value his senses (what he feels) over his mental image (what he thinks) in making a decision.

When he is unable to do this, he is referred to another department. The escalator seems to be saying that this process of transcendence or learning could be effortless if the dreamer could surrender to it. The dream then suggests that the dreamer is tempted to back out and avoid making a choice again. If he was allowed to get off the escalator and keep moving, the dream might be suggesting that it was okay to avoid making the choice. But the dream figure of the crow, a cunning and crafty bird, does not want the man to avoid the decision. Everything conspires in the dream to move the dreamer toward making a decision.

Like a myth or heroic tale, this man is on a quest. His magical powers are recognized by others (his perceptual abilities as he describes his wife are praised by the salesperson) at the same time that he is given a test that would confirm or bestow new powers on him (choosing perfume based on his senses). He meets two allies (the courage and willingness to run counter to the accepted path and a kind of crafty or even tricky intelligence) in the form of the salesperson and the crow. He perseveres, has his moment of doubt, but is held by fate to his course.

Having gotten this far in opening up a dream is often far enough. The first three sets of questions would be considered part of the diagnostic process. The remaining questions link the dream to specific issues in the dreamer's life and look at what the dream suggests in order to rebalance the energy.

Fourth Stone Question
(Everything Is Connected)

How am I connected to this dream,
or how does this dream connect to my life?

We began this process by moving back from the personal imagery to the archetypal imagery. Now we want to see how the dream is related to specific issues in the dreamer's life.

The dreamer shared that he had been worried about how he was going to do the things his career required without upsetting his wife. They might have to relocate if he was going to advance. He had not discussed this with his wife because he believed he knew what her answer would be. She often talked about how much she liked her home, her career, and the area they lived in, so he assumed that she would either refuse to move or resent him deeply for making them move. As he shared this, he realized that even in the dream the impulse to buy his wife a gift was to put her in a good mood and to talk to her about this issue.

Fifth Stone Question (Everything Responds)

What does the dream suggest I do to move
the stuck energy and reestablish sacred relationship?

We talked about the events and imagery in the dream and what they suggested to the dreamer. One of the first things he noticed was that his assumption that his wife would not agree to the move was based on a mental perception of her. This perception, while it contributed to the current conflict, was an image that he was otherwise completely comfortable with. He also realized that there was risk involved in seeing her in a different way. They had been high school sweethearts, had married young, and had not changed their expectations of each other even though they had both undergone profound changes in the 11 years of their marriage. He expressed that the job issue was probably bigger than he had admitted to himself previously. It had the capacity to shake up a lot of things and test how committed they both were to remaining in the relationship. He returned to his answer to the question of what wanted to happen in the dream, and we discussed what a gift it would be to give his wife a chance to be seen in a fresh way, the way she is today, not the way she was in high school.

He also identified a tendency to avoid making choices and to either choose what seemed to be the most popular or accepted path (according to parents, friends, and colleagues) or to make no choice and just wait for things to be thrust upon him. During our discussion he even questioned whether the career move was what he really wanted, seeing it more as the choice he was supposed to want. He certainly did not want to sit passively by while his marriage deteriorated. In the end, the dreamer embraced the energy of the dream characters that seemed to be supporting him in the risk of trusting his own feelings. He liked the punk salesperson and even said she reminded him of the kind of person he had wished he could have been like when he was younger.

There are many ways to do dreamwork. This process is a good way to unfold a dream while staying true to the dreamspirits and the dreamstory. Remaining true to the dreamspirits and the dreamstory is a way of engaging the unseen world based on respect. It is relatively straightforward and doesn't require special skills other than careful attention to detail and pattern.

Why These Questions?

The connection between the principles of the Five Stones and the questions we ask of the dream is easy enough to remember.

Because *everything is alive,* every figure or object in my dream can be thought of as a character or dreamspirit. The best way to understand why Spirit chose to use these specific dreamspirits in a dream is to study them, ask questions about them, and understand the nature of the forms they are taking. So I ask what they are and what are their qualities and their distinctions. I also identify the field by asking where the dream occurs and what my sense of time is. Sometimes a dreamer will not remember a place or have no sense of time. That detail is as important as anything they might remember and will be woven into the energetic story. In long dreams where the setting shifts sharply, consider breaking the dream down into segments based on location. As long as the dream's location doesn't change, consider that one act of the dream. When it does shift, consider that a second act. If there is a third change of location, even if it is a return to a previous location, that would be a separate act in the dream. Multiple locations can signal an evolutionary process or the need to consider the dream issue in a variety of settings in one's life.

If *everything is conscious,* I can consider what the dreamspirits of my dream want. I can also enter into dialogue with them. So I ask what they want, what would fulfill their soul purpose, and, in a larger sense, what wants to happen in the dream. If this seems hard or foolish, remember that this process requires the right balance of respect and playfulness. Don't settle for just one answer to these questions. Give yourself several possibilities to choose from. If you can't think of totally different answers, try out different wordings so you have several flavors of the same answer. I can also choose to reenter a dream or invoke a dream character or even become lucid (wake up) within a dream.

If *everything moves,* if it is in the nature of healthy systems to move and transform, I can look for examples of movement in my dream. Is it upward, downward, or lateral movement? Am I flying, floating, surfing, sailing, swimming, rolling, skating, driving, or riding? Each of these ways of moving and methods of being moved have their own energy. What else moves in my dream? What gets stuck in my dream? Where and how am I prohibited from moving? Is there a conflict or clash of energies, and does it create movement or stuckness? Is the movement threatening, or is the sense of being stuck threatening?

If *everything is connected,* I can see the dream or even several dream fragments as being related. I can ask how one part of a dream connects to another, even if the elements seem disparate. I can ask how a dream connects to my life or how I am currently acting out the dreamstory in my waking life. I can also consider the dreams of close friends and family members and ask how they are related to my situation. There have been documented studies that show that when a group of people decides to dream together for an individual or for the collective, the dream images overlap in a way that is well beyond what might be expected by chance.

If *everything responds,* I can ask what the dream I had is in response to. To which issue or worry or request for guidance did this dream come in answer? Some dreams seem only to illuminate a problem and are in that sense only diagnostic dreams. Most dreams, however, contain the seed of rebalance. We get clear guidance about what we need to do to rebalance the energy and return to a healthy relationship.

Now how about your own dreams? Practice this technique with one of your recent dreams. Look for the energetic pattern that you are enacting in your waking life. This is not an idle exercise to be done just for the sake of curiosity. Your nightly expeditions into the dreamworld can help you correct your course and regain your balance on a daily basis.

There have been times when I have slighted someone in a dream and felt compelled to apologize to them in waking life. At first, this was rather awkward. As I began to trust it, however, I discovered that my dreamspirits were usually correct. Either I actually had slighted the person unknowingly and they were repressing the sense of being hurt (not good for them or me) or some imbalance actually existed from an event neither of us could recall and the ensuing conversation rebalanced the relationship.

Dreams can illuminate your soul's path. They can shine a light on the events of the next day, week, month, or year. And, though they may initially seem confusing, if we spend a little time connecting with the dreamspirits and the dreamstory, they speak to us with a beautiful and poetic kind of clarity.

Now that you have a sense of what kind of guidance and support you can find on your soul path through dreams, wouldn't it be nice to focus that power? You can learn to dream the answers to questions the same way shamans do and our Stone Age ancestors did.

Seeking guidance through dreams is an incubation process. Like any kind of journey into an altered state of consciousness, a dream journey benefits from clarity and compassion. Clarity means that we know what we want to have answered, and probably why. Compassion means that we will be patient with both the answers and the possible lack of answers.

In Ancient Greece, people sought healing dreams in the temples of the god Aesculapius. They would prepare themselves with ritual baths, fasting or special diets, periods of meditation or contemplation, and prayer. Once their intentions were properly focused, the dreamer would sleep in a specially prepared chamber, ready to receive the healing wisdom of the gods through dreams.

◈ STONE AGE WISDOM PRACTICE #3:

Dream Incubation for Guidance

Consider the following guidelines to help you prepare and focus your dreaming:

• Allow yourself a few minutes to sit with your shaman's traveling journal before going to bed. Spend some time writing about the issue that you want assistance with. If it's a personal issue, describe it and describe how you feel about it.

• Write the next day's date at the top of the page and state as clearly as possible your question or what it is you would like to receive from the spirit world through your dreams. If you are aware of specific dreamspirits that have been helpful in the past, invoke their assistance.

• While it is possible to ask big questions like, "What should I do with my life?" and "Why am I here?" sometimes it's more productive to take smaller bites. Ask for guidance rather than answers. Instead of asking, "Which job offer should I choose?" try asking, "What do I need to know or do in order to make the best choice between these two jobs?"

• As you fall asleep, repeat your question or request over and over again as a mantra.

• Record whatever you remember of your dreams upon waking, even if it does not seem instantly relevant. It may take several tries to get clear guidance, but stick with it. Once you've developed the ability to program your dreaming consciousness, you'll have a constant connection to specific spiritual guidance.

Dream incubation seems to respond well to sensory immersion. At a retreat in Mexico, workshop participants gathered around a beautiful tile pool after dark. We had placed votive candles around the edge of the pool so that flickering candlelight and moonlight were the only forms of illumination. We lit fragrant incense, had soft music playing, and encouraged participants to sit on the edge of the pool with their feet dangling in the warm water. The intention behind the experience was to help workshop participants move out of their daily experience of the world and into sacred space and time, and to connect with the element of water in their dreams. Shamanic practitioner Kelly Leigh told an African folk tale about making the descent into water, followed by a simple meditation exercise. When we finished, we invited participants to move quietly to bed to dream.

The dreams of the next morning were rich with water imagery and the themes of descent and submersion.

Consider giving yourself the gift of a sensual dream-guidance focusing ceremony. Draw a bath and scent it with fragrant oils, light candles, and put on your favorite music. Lie back and imagine yourself moving through the dreamworld, gathering the wisdom and guidance you need. Create a small altar of sacred objects beside your bed, especially those that relate to the issue you are dreaming on. Make an offering of cornmeal or tobacco or clear spirits to the Earth. Finally, go to bed full of the intention to dream.

Medicine Dreams

While all dreams can be unfolded to reveal something useful about our current relationship to the unseen world, some dreams are especially important and deserve special attention. In Tuva, the shamans pay extra attention to dreams in which deceased ancestors appear. Among the Inuit, dreams of specific sea creatures are considered especially important. Shamans in most traditions consider dreams of death to be initiatory. These kinds of special dreams are sometimes called Medicine Dreams, and they tell us about our power. If you need to make choices about the time you spend attending to the meaning of your dreams, let this list help you prioritize.

Some of the characteristics of Medicine Dreams include:
- the presence of wild, mythical, or unusual animals;
- deceased relatives and ancestors who provide specific guidance;
- mentor figures that communicate in clear, specific language;
- cross-cultural spirit guides;
- mythical or fantastic beings;
- historical or fantastic settings;

- the experience of flight;
- the experience of breathing underwater;
- deaths, transformations, and "magical" events;
- new rituals, songs, or guidance in the alteration of a ceremony.

Take your Medicine Dreams seriously, but don't let them go to your head. Medicine Dreams are not better than other dreams, and having Medicine Dreams does not necessarily make you a better or more spiritually evolved person.

The Lenape tribe in North America have a word they call *Maskan,* which translates to "Medicine" or "Spiritual Power." For the Lenape, having a Medicine Dream is the first step in acquiring Maskan. Bringing a Maskan or Medicine Dream to a Lenape elder would simply mean that you now had the chance to prove that you can actually carry the gift of Maskan into the waking world. In the words of the Native American Elder Sun Bear, "Don't tell me about your visions unless they can grow corn."

Before I close this chapter, I'd like to stress again the importance of the kinds of questions we learned to ask about our dreams. Applying these questions and an attitude of respectful observation and study to the phenomena we encounter in the work of vision-shifting, journeying, shape-shifting, conducting ceremony, and creating will open up the hidden energetic fields and patterns of the unseen world faster than anything I know.

Stone Age Wisdom Principles

Principle #1: The First Stone

Everything is alive.

Everything has its own living spirit.

Primal Alignment: Study

We learn to be observant.

We learn to pay attention.

We learn to look and listen, to see things as they are,

to learn the true nature of things.

The Dreamer's Questions:

What is it?

What makes it distinctive?

Where or in what field is it occurring?

What is the thing in itself, before the imposition

of my opinions and attitudes about it?

Shamanic Practice:

Vision-shifting

CHAPTER 4

Vision-Shifting: Seeing the Unseen World

*We may at first have trouble trying to visualize a
rock or an atom as a living thing because we associate
consciousness with life. But this notion is just a
human limitation; a rock may also have difficulty
in understanding human consciousness.*

Itzhak Bentov,
*Stalking the Wild Pendulum:
On the Mechanics of Consciousness*

ONCE UPON A TIME WE SPENT our nights gathered around fires. The
world by firelight is a very different place from the world as seen
by electric light. By fire, everything seems to move. Shadows and
light dance across stone and bush. Forms emerge from stone as
the flames shift. When we move around a fire, we seem to move
in relationship to the way the shadows are dancing. By firelight, it
is easy to see that the world is alive.

Every good teacher knows the difference between telling a student an answer and having that student discover the answer for him or herself. One of the distinctions I make between a client and student is that a client usually wants relief of symptoms, whereas a student knows he or she wants to make a life change. If a client comes to me with a problem, I will provide whatever meaning and diagnosis I can from what *I* see. When working with a student, it is important that he or she develop his or her *own* ability to see.

Zach, a young man who had begun studying with me, asked about why he kept injuring his right ankle over and over again. He felt it had some significance, but he couldn't identify the cause. I could look at him energetically. I could seek information from my spirit guides. I could tell him what was wrong, but he had come to me as a student, and he needed to discover for himself the unseen or energetic causes for the repeated trauma to his ankle.

To see more deeply into the energetic nature of this recurring situation, I treated the injury the same way I would treat an event in dreamtime. I asked the same questions in the same order that I would ask of a dreamspirit. I asked Zach to think about what an ankle was. We agreed that it was a joint that articulates the motion of the foot. While you don't need an ankle to walk, it does help you walk smoothly and gracefully, and it helps you keep your balance. It is also the place through which all the nerves and blood supply of the foot must pass. I asked if there was a difference between the right ankle and the left ankle. He thought about it for a while and commented that when he started walking, he always stepped out with his right foot. I inquired about the nature of the injury. It had always been sprained, never broken. We agreed that a sprain was usually caused by the overextension of a joint—moving it in a strange new direction or moving it further than it was used to moving. I asked him what an ankle wants out of life. Though this is an odd question, it often produces illuminating answers. After some thought, he said that an ankle wants to remain flexible and strong, to allow information to flow between the foot and the body, and to not go off in new directions too suddenly.

Next I asked him to focus on what he had been doing, thinking, and feeling before each injury. This was a difficult question that took some time to think about. The only thing he could recall was that two of the injuries had actually interfered with trips he had planned. The first was with a girl he had just met and the second was for a job interview. I asked him what the injury had kept him from doing. He admitted that the first injury probably kept him from getting involved with someone he shouldn't have (the girl went on the trip anyway, with another man). The second injury meant he did not get a chance at a job he had wanted.

I could have stopped there, as some patterns were already emerging. When Zach's dreambody (the energetic template for his physical body) picked up signals from the soul that something was happening too fast or moving in the wrong direction, the ankle was given the task of slowing Zach down. I could have left it at that, but this was a good way to practice the skills of vision-shifting, so I encouraged Zach to work with this issue through some other channels.

I asked him to program his dreams to reveal an answer. He dreamed of trying to get control of a runaway lawn mower. I asked him to lie quietly and move his consciousness into his ankle, and then to be open to whatever images or sensory experiences came up. He reported seeing his alcoholic and abusive father fall down the stairs and break his ankle, remembering that he felt safe for the first time when his father was in bed in a cast. He also remembered trying to jump from a brick wall that his brother had jumped from and injuring his right ankle when he was seven years old. He felt a heaviness in his heart and a kind of fear that he identified as the fear of being left behind.

We worked to sensitize his hands to "feel" the energy moving through his body—where it was blocked and where it was escaping. He developed a kind of stretching practice that involved running his energized hands down his legs and around his ankles to his feet, with the intention of developing physical and energetic strength and flexibility.

I taught him how to ask his soul about his ankle through prayer and how to attend to the answer through the images in a stone. Through all these practices and channels of information, we wove together a story about his injuring his ankle that told of both his desire to move forward and his fear of being left behind. Realizing that he had come to associate safety with immobility was a revelation for this otherwise active young man. Once he knew the story, he knew what to do to set the intention for moving forward through ceremony. We created a ritual in which he rewrote his soul contract and agreed that in exchange for his ankle not being used as the dreambody's messenger, he would pay closer attention to the messages that came through his dreams.

Carl Jung once observed, "The Gods have become diseases." For the shaman, there is an angel or spirit in every illness. James Hillman writes, "To see the angel in the malady requires an eye for the invisible, a certain blinding of one eye and an opening of the other to elsewhere…Even in the sciences, you only begin to see the phenomenon in the sky or under the microscope if someone first describes what you are looking for; we need instruction in the art of seeing. Then the invisible becomes suddenly visible, right in your squinting eye."

What the student of shamanism tries to develop is an alternative capacity for paying attention. Our most common form of attention is when we focus on the primary processes of everyday reality. When we use this attention, we try to understand what people mean based on what they say. When we use a secondary level of attention, we don't disregard what they say, but we focus on the double signals we pick up. Double signals reveal themselves through body language and the odd perceptions that we normally consider to be just chance or accident. The ability to perceive through this second attention is what I call vision-shifting. It's the art of paying attention in a sacred manner.

Vision-shifting helps us see or become sensitive to the unseen world. The techniques help us sense the "aliveness" of the world around us. The shaman doesn't *trust* that the world is alive, conscious, dynamic, connected, and responsive—he *knows* it, because it is what he sees and experiences. The shaman or shamanic practitioner doesn't accept things on faith, but rather encounters them experientially.

Vision-shifting is altering one's sensory resonance to be able to see, feel, smell, hear, or even taste the unseen world. It is attention to the unusual events that occur in and around us—the sudden emergence of a clear pattern in a chaotic moment, the synchronous timing of a bird calling or flying through an open window, the odd disruption that breaks the predictable pattern, the slip of the tongue or the cough that is out of place. These are not such unusual experiences. They happen to each of us every day. In little moments, we perceive things differently. We notice things we had not noticed. The difference is that for the shaman, these things have significance. They are messages, glimpses of the implicit order of the field in which a drama is unfolding. The shaman is one who uses discipline, practice, and intention to extend her vision into the energetic realm. Vision-shifting combines the first attention to everyday reality with the second attention to the dreaming reality.

The second time I encountered Gray Morning Bear was not in a journey but in a dream. He did not take the form of a North American native elder, but of an old, white-haired electrician. Still, it was clear in the dream and after I awoke that they were merely different outer forms for the same guiding spirit.

I am in a room in an old house. There is not enough furniture to determine what the purpose of the room is, but there are five floor lamps and some wooden chairs. I am standing. An old man that I know is an electrician is sitting in one of the chairs. He says that the problem with this room is that there are a lot of lamps but not much light. I turn the switch on one of the lights and it comes on.

"Well, that was easy," he says, "but there still isn't enough light." I turn the switch on another lamp and nothing happens. I look down and notice that the lamp is not plugged in. I plug it in and the light comes on.

"Good," the old man nods, "but the room would be happier with more light." I try another lamp but it fails to come on. I check the plug and it is plugged in. I try plugging one of the working lamps into the outlet and now the working lamp fails to light. "So now what do you do?" the old man asks.

I realize that this is a kind of lesson or test for me. "Well," I say, "the outlet doesn't seem to have power. A wire must be cut somewhere. We could rewire it."

"You know a lot of people don't believe in electricity. Do you?"

"Of course," I answer.

"Well, where is this electricity? Can you see it?"

"You can't see it, but it's all around us. It's moving through the walls."

"Well, all I'm saying is that if you didn't believe in this electricity, solving the light problem would be pretty confusing." As he says this I realize I can actually see through the walls. I can see the trail of electricity pulsing along the wires. I can see where it comes from and where it goes. I can see it circulating. I can see where it stops flowing. I laugh and wake up.

As I thought about this dream over the next couple of days, I realized that people are a lot like the lamps in the room. Sometimes we just aren't turned on; we're not connected to a real purpose. Other times we want to turn on, but we aren't connected to a source of power. If we understand or believe in electricity, the problem of reconnecting or rewiring becomes simple. If we don't understand or believe in electricity, we end up concluding that the ability to shine is a gift some people have and others don't. With first attention we see what is on the surface rather than what is behind the walls. Second attention is like my being able to see the electricity moving through the walls. Vision-shifting is a combination of both ways of perceiving.

Realizing Our Energy

Our energy, our electricity, comes from the universal life force around us. This force gives us the energy to manifest healthy bodies, maintain healthy relationships, think, love, create, work, play, and follow our soul paths. It is the power with which we are meant to not just live our lives, but to shine. In the process of living life, it is normal to lose the balance between the amount of energy you are taking in and the amount you are expending, but we are not supposed to be living long periods of time in energy debt. Our bodies get sick, our relationships deteriorate, we lose the capacity to experience joy, and we are unable to complete our soul tasks.

The odd thing is that we are literally swimming in an inexhaustible sea of energy, but most of us fail to tap into it. We don't replenish our supply for a number of reasons.

We don't believe in this energy. We can't see it. Doctors, scientists, and the culture we live in don't acknowledge or accept it. We don't understand the energetic significance of right relationship, and we assume that we're isolated and on our own.

We don't understand how to tap into the energy. No one has ever taught us about personal energy management and maintenance.

Our energetic systems are damaged in such a way that we cannot receive the energy we need. It's as if our wires are crossed, broken, or missing.

Perhaps one of the most important ways in which vision-shifting and embracing the shamanic view of a living, conscious, dynamic, connected, and responsive world helps one return to balance is that we begin to be able to see or sense our own energetic patterns, the energetic patterns of those around us, and the energy that is actually available to us.

When people speak of shamanism they usually associate it with journeys into imaginal realms facilitated by the ingestion of psychoactive substances or trance-inducing practices. While this is a very real part of shamanism, most of the shamans I have come in contact with spend far less time out of their bodies and far more time deeply inhabiting their bodies. They operate in a vision-shifted state of consciousness that allows them to live and function in the material world while being constantly open to information from the unseen world. This is an ability that can be developed to a greater or lesser degree by anyone. Vision-shifting means you have the option of seeing the same scene from two vantage points.

Becoming the Hunter

Shamans evolved in hunter-gatherer cultures and the hunter's skills are essential to shamanic practice. Courage and the strength to persevere, compassionate reverence for life, the ability to navigate, patience, intuition, and careful attention to detail and pattern are what make hunters successful. Careful attention to detail and pattern requires a way of seeing that is both focused and diffuse. The hunter must follow a specific trail and at the same time be constantly aware of the surrounding environment. The shamans of Peru say that once you embark on a spirit path, the Tirakuna or "the Watchers" begin to stalk you. Being watched reminds us to be watchers ourselves. As urban contemporary shamanic practitioners, we learn from our Stone Age ancestors that what we do not actively hunt and seek to know may actually end up hunting us.

In the classical world, a talent or gift was considered to be a daimon or spirit possessing or acting through an individual. The Christian church would later corrupt daimon into demon, but originally there was no negative connotation attached to the term daimon. This is not to say that daimons could not wreak havoc in the lives of individuals. Denying a daimon or ignoring it was a recipe for disaster. Thinking about it this way, we understand why shamans describe their work as hunting. They are hunting power. A talent or gift is a form of power. If we do not stalk and hunt it, it will turn and hunt us. An artist not making art will find just as much creative capacity turned against her—working to disrupt her life and plans. A healer not healing often finds the daimon of healing is just as capable of bringing illness and disease. If you deny your power, it will suck the energy it needs from you anyway, and you will feel drained, depressed, and disoriented.

Arnold Mindell writes in *The Shaman's Body: A New Shamanism for Transforming Health, Relationships, and the Community*, "As a hunter you must study the rational details of energy, of 'psychic prey.' You are doing more than just learning about the signals of the unknown. You are developing the ability to notice and to follow signs that give greater access to life, to the energy that makes every moment exciting and awesome. You are waiting to gain the courage to drop your ordinary way of living."

The hunters of flesh and blood animals recognize the signs of their prey. Shamans learn to recognize the signs of their psychic or energetic prey. The shaman attends to perceptual irregularities—whether they form interesting patterns or break patterns. They attend to visual and auditory signals that no one else may perceive. They may refer to their prey as spirits, energies, guides, demons, or angels. Their prey can harm or heal. The shaman learns to hunt situations that are unusual, to seek the objects of power, to stalk the mystery. That vague sensation, odd feeling, intuitive hit, or strange thought is the sign of the nearness of your energetic prey as surely as the fresh tracks, warm scat, or sudden flight of birds tells the hunter how close he is to the lion.

"It is time to reclaim our inner hunter," writes contemporary shaman Evelyn Rysdyk in her book, *Modern Shamanic Living: New Explorations of an Ancient Path.* When you have developed your hunting ability—the power to see, listen, and feel from a deeper awareness—your prey will always be just a vision-shift away in any situation.

Since so much emphasis is placed on the visual in our culture, we'll begin with some vision-shifting techniques for expanding your ability to see. These exercises use imagination to improve your range of vision.

❖ STONE AGE WISDOM PRACTICE #4:
Vision Walk
In order to practice vision walking, you need to learn how to soften and open up your focus. This way of seeing allows you to be open and sensitive to visual clues. It is the way Aborigines move through the landscape, acknowledging the spirits of place around them. It is the way our Stone Age ancestors were able to survive the dangers around them while taking advantage of the opportunities to find food, medicine, and tools.

Begin by finding a place outdoors to stand or sit in a relaxed posture. Look at the horizon and squint your eyes softly. Alter your focus as if you were shifting a camera from normal to panoramic view. Think of your vision as being wide and diffuse. Try to relax the muscles around your eyes while still maintaining this expanded field of view. Avoid focusing your attention on any one point of the horizon or foreground. Take it all in. If you find yourself focusing on a specific object, let it go and return to your softened general field of view. Practice holding this kind of attention until you can do it for several minutes at a time. When your vision is shifted in this way, you may begin to notice movement, glowing light, or flashes that draw your attention, but, when you focus on them, you find there's nothing there. This experience is rather like watching a pond for jumping fish. You may see a fish jump in your peripheral vision, but by the time you focus on it, the fish is gone. If you try to look for the spot where the fish will jump next, you will always be off. But if you soften your gaze and widen your field of view, you will see the fish jump.

Once you can sit with this kind of vision, try walking with it. Ask a question about something that has been concerning you. Evoke your expanded vision and go for a walk. Pay specific attention to the things that jump, pop, or move as you walk. It is nice to do this in a natural setting, but it isn't essential. A simple walk around the block will do.

Let's imagine I've been pondering whether or not to accept a new job, and I have asked for guidance. As I soften my focus and walk, I am immediately aware of a flock of black birds rising up from a tree to my far right as if spooked by something. Next, my attention is captured by a driver honking impatiently at the driver ahead when the light has turned green and the front car has not moved. Finally, I notice the glare of reflected sunlight off the windows of an office building. I pay attention to what the office building is and note that it is empty now, but that it used to be a bank. The bank's slogan, "Get what you want today," is still stenciled on the window. I weave these images together with my question and situation. I know I don't want to be scared or spooked into taking a new job. I also know that while I don't want to drag my feet and miss an opportunity to change direction, I don't want to act impatiently, either. There also seems to be a warning in the sign that suggests that I can get what I want today. I don't believe it is healthy to focus only on my short-term goals. It didn't seem to serve the bank well.

It is easy to argue that I'm not learning anything I didn't already know, but most of the time we do know the answers we need. Using our first attention, however, leaves us confused by the number of choices we have. Using our second attention brings an awareness of which choice most aligns with our soul's purpose.

◈ STONE AGE WISDOM PRACTICE #5:

Shifting Your Attention

Have you ever wished you could see behind you or beyond your field of view? Well, shamans learn this kind of seeing by moving their consciousness, the center of their perception, outside their bodies. This is not as difficult or strange as it may sound. I'm sure you've had the experience of being in a crowded room filled with conversations and suddenly you hear your name spoken from across the room. It wasn't that your name was shouted. It's just that your name is a particular sound pattern you are sensitive to. You resonate with it. Or perhaps you've felt someone watching you, even if you couldn't see anyone in your immediate field of vision. These are examples of our ability to shift our perceptual consciousness.

You can practice this exercise almost anywhere. First, imagine that your conscious awareness is a little bubble not much bigger than a golf ball. You can imagine this as the third eye inside your head. (The third eye is your higher psychic or spiritual form of vision and is usually thought to be located inside the head, at the forehead, between the eyebrows.) Close your eyes and imagine this bubble floating inside your head. Use the bubble, rather than your eyes, to perceive the room in front of you. Recreate the room in your imagination. Do not open your eyes. If you cannot remember a detail, let the bubble move outside your head to explore the room. Send the bubble out to your sides and behind you. Where is the furniture? Who is behind you? Who is to the side? Try allowing the bubble to float over your head and slowly spin to take in the full room. Try sending the bubble around corners.

At first it will seem like you are just imagining what you are seeing. This is fine. Shifting your perception is a new ability and takes some practice to get used to. If you have trouble visualizing the room, do you find that you hear a voice describing what is around you? If so, you may have a stronger auditory channel, which will respond well to the next part of this exercise. If you neither see nor hear particularly well, monitor your body's physical sensations. Do you feel pain, heat, coolness, tingling, buzzing, discomfort, or any change in your body's steady state when you send your awareness outside of yourself? If so, you may have a particularly strong kinesthetic receptor channel. Visual, auditory, and kinesthetic channels can all be excellent sources of the kind of information you will need to gather as a hunter of power. Don't give up on any one channel too soon. Many people have strong primary channels but also good secondary channels. Eventually you will find that you can sense what you cannot see with your waking-world eyes.

To continue this exercise, pull your conscious awareness bubble back inside your head. Now listen. What can you hear around you? What is the closest sound to you? Now slowly begin to expand the bubble inside your head as if it were a "third ear" instead of a "third eye." Be aware of when the bubble encompasses the source of a particular sound. Blow the bubble up until you can hear sounds that are farther and farther away. What is the farthest sound you can hear? Once you have that sound within your bubble, allow your consciousness to shift to that place. Look back at yourself or at least in your direction. How far away are you? What is between your consciousness and your body? Move your awareness back to your body in a straight line. What did you encounter? Where did you go? What did it feel like?

Practice this important technique playfully and frequently. It can make boring and unproductive moments, such as waiting on line or riding the subway, into psychic and energetic hunting expeditions.

◈ STONE AGE WISDOM PRACTICE #6:

Seeing Between

Once you can move your consciousness outside your body or at least expand the range of your awareness, you are ready to try seeing between. This technique for vision-shifting comes from the Celtic tradition of honoring the points betwixt and between two things. For the Celtic shamans, places where two elements such as water and earth or fire and water came together were places where magic was most likely to occur.

The experience of vision-shifting is one of finding oneself in the waking world one moment and in the dreaming world the next. It is a feeling of being between two places—as if dancing on the borders of reality. Vision-shifting through this kind of border dance is an excellent way to take a compass reading on your direction in the middle of a busy day or to find the energetic field in which you are currently operating. It can help you tap the intuition of your dreaming mind at a moment's notice.

Vision-shifting in its most spontaneous form comes over us with little intention on our part, but we can experience it more willfully. Begin by finding a liminal point. (Liminal points are points of energetic or elemental transition, such as the boundary between water and land or earth and sky.) Once you are practiced at it, you will find liminal points all around you. Find a comfortable place where you can sit for a while, and focus your attention on the point in between two things. With a tree, this might mean the point between roots and earth or leaves and sky. At the seashore, this might be the point between wave and sand or ocean spray and sky. Try not to focus on either single element, but on the point between them.

Stay with it. Imagine yourself into this space. Spend as much time in this space as you can before being pulled out by distractions. Pay attention to the images and the body sensations that come to you while in this between space. Move your attention into the body sensations you experience. Imagine your attention as being a small, transparent bubble of awareness that you can shift effortlessly into these between spaces or into areas of your body. Let this bubble track or hunt for you, following the bodily sensations wherever they may lead.

For example, as I sit and focus my attention between the water and the stone in a small fountain, I find myself aware of the coolness of the water and the feeling of it sheeting over the stone. I also feel the slippery smoothness of the stone. I allow my consciousness to move closer and closer to the absolute middle ground—the place that is neither fully stone nor fully water. In so doing, I become aware of an itching or tingling inside my ears and at the back of my neck. I shift my bubble of attention to that point and track the sensation. I'm aware that the sensation is the same feeling I get when I believe people are talking about me behind my back. I track this sensation and realize that I am worried about what other people are saying about me. Next I imagine what they might be saying about me that I would find disagreeable. Whatever it is, I amplify it. Instead of repressing it, I embrace it. I move into it. I embrace the disagreeable me, the unattractive me, the "less than perfect" me. I hold my attention there—feeling the feelings without the need to act on them or do anything about them. Within moments the negative feelings begin to dissipate, and I find myself able to move back to the water and the stone. I do this whether I feel I have the time or not, because it allows me to express gratitude to the water and the stone. Leaving the way I entered also makes it easier to find my way back later.

You may find this practice awkward at first, but give it a try. There will come a moment when you experience a shift in awareness. Things will become clearer, more alive, and more intense. In the beginning it may not last long, but you can learn to slip into these spaces of *no time* at will.

◈ STONE AGE WISDOM PRACTICE #7:

The Strong Eye

In Australia, the Aborigines speak of a kind of seeing they call "the strong eye." This is a kind of X-ray vision by which a shaman can see into a person to diagnose disease or dysfunction. While vision walking requires a kind of softening of vision, the Strong Eye requires a laserlike focusing of vision. It involves seeing with the third eye and is useful for determining the true nature of a thing.

First, find a stone that is about the size of your hand and locate a clock or watch that you can use to time yourself for three minutes. You can do this exercise with any small object, if a stone is too hard to find.

Find a quiet time when you will not be interrupted. Turn off the television and radio. Set your stone in front of you on a bare surface and against a background that offers few distractions. Now, discipline yourself to observe your stone for a full three minutes. Study the surface of your stone. You can turn it over and around in your hand. Really look at it. If your mind wanders, gently bring it back to observing the stone.

What we are attempting to do in this three minutes of intense observation is to bore our rational mind and trick it into shutting down for a moment. The rational mind doesn't really see. The rational mind has learned to value efficiency over accuracy. It considers real attention to detail a waste of time. Its function is to look long enough to identify and classify. Then it can move on to something else, leaving a kind of visual cliché in the place occupied by the object. This is a useful ability. It allows us to perform complex tasks quickly, but it also keeps us from really seeing what we look at. A particular stone becomes a category called "stone-like objects." A radiant human being is reduced to a category called "woman," "Asian," or an even more vague but debilitating category like "other," "foreign," or "strange."

The kind of clear sight we are trying to develop here is similar to what Yogic and some Buddhist practitioners call third eye sight. This involves opening the third eye. In these practices, it is the third eye that sees what is really there—that shatters the illusion created by the rational mind.

The best way to know that you've accomplished this task of opening up to a different way of seeing is to experience the shift, meaning that the thing you are observing will suddenly shift in your hand. It might actually feel like movement, or it might be a kind of visual intensification. This is hard to put into words

because we don't have precise language for this kind of experience. It's as if a thing becomes more itself than it was a moment
before. If you are observing a stone, it will become more richly
itself. You will notice patterns and textures you hadn't seen. Some
people describe their objects as suddenly becoming more beautiful
or more fascinating. Sometimes this shift comes over you suddenly,
sometimes the change is more gradual, but either way, stay with
the exercise for at least three minutes. Even if the shift is not dramatic,
you will notice new things about your object. The more you practice,
the easier it will be to open your strong eye.

◈ STONE AGE WISDOM PRACTICE #8:
Hunting for Signs of Life
Remember that vision-shifting combines first attention to everyday
reality with second-level attention to the dreaming reality. It is a
way to come to know the fundamental aliveness of the universe
around you by experiencing it firsthand. What the shaman experiences
is that the universe, as reflected in the objects around us, is a tool
for divination. Ask a question of any object, and you will find an
answer. In this exercise, we will hunt for signs of life in a simple
stone, but any object that's available could work.

Perhaps you are looking for guidance on a particular issue.
First spend a moment clarifying your question. Next, select a small
stone (not larger than your fist), your shaman's traveling journal,
and some colored pencils or markers. Sketch an outline of the
stone in the center of a page of your journal, leaving enough room
around the edges to add some writing. You may want to flip the
stone over and trace an outline from the back, as well.

Begin to inspect the stone. Look for a pattern or marking on
the stone that looks like an image. You may see animals, objects,

people, landscapes, words, letters, or symbols. Draw what you see in your journal and annotate it with any words or phrases that come to you. Stop and disconnect from this image. Close your eyes, take a deep breath, exhale, and open your eyes again. Find a second image in the stone. Perform this process a total of five times.

Now you have five images that have valuable information about the issue on which you were seeking guidance. Ask of the five images the same kinds of questions you learned to ask of your dreamspirits in chapter 2. What is it? What does it want? What does it have to tell me? Is anything stuck or moving in a distinctive way? How do these images weave together into a story that relates to the question I was asking? What course of action does this suggest?

You can also hunt for signs of life by learning to sense and listen to objects. Take a break and wash and dry your hands. This is a kind of ritual act that focuses your attention on what you are about to do. Next, you will need to sensitize your hands. Clap your hands together sharply one or more times. Shake your hands loosely until your fingers begin to feel limp. Finally, rub your palms together in a circular motion until you feel the heat of friction building up between them. When your hands feel ready (hot and open), hold them 5 or 6 inches apart, palms facing toward each other, as if you were holding an invisible melon. Become aware of the energy between your hands. You may feel a tingling in your palms or fingertips. It may feel stronger in one hand than in the other. It might feel like an itch or it might seem like an elastic cord connecting palm to palm or fingertips to fingertips.

You may find it easy to sense this kind of energetic field or you may have to practice a bit more, but everyone is capable of it. If you practice it often enough, you may not need to prepare your hands in any way before beginning to perceive the energetic field.

Now place the stone on the palm of one hand and cup the other hand over it.

Pay attention to the feeling in your hands. What should you expect to feel? Well, if this is new to you, you might feel a little silly. If you don't feel something immediate and dramatic, you might be tempted to dismiss the whole experience or to conclude that you have no ability. Stay with the experience a while longer. Do your hands itch or tingle? Sometimes stones will feel warmer than you expect them to. Sometimes they will be cooler. How do your palms feel?

While focusing on the feeling in your hands, begin asking a series of "What does it want?" questions. As you ask these questions, be aware of the thoughts, images, and impressions that come to you. Do sudden strong images come to your mind? Do you recognize the images from your life, or are they new to you? Open yourself up to these images, but don't linger on them. For now it is enough to note the images the stone triggers.

Ask yourself the following questions:
   1. *What is my first impression of this stone?*
   2. *Where has this stone been?*
   3. *Who has held this stone?*
   4. *Why has this stone come to me?*

Write down the answers to these questions in your journal. Don't censor yourself. Trust your first impressions. If you hear a dialogue, write it down. Don't try to interpret anything, just record your impressions.

As a final question, ask the stone for its name.

You can use the techniques described above to do a reading for yourself or others when questions arise. You can use a stone, a leaf, or almost any found object, though natural objects seem to work better. If you are reading for someone else, have him or her bring the object to be read. Sensitize your hands while focusing on the question that is being asked. Study the object carefully and locate three patterns or pictures contained within the object. (If you are reading for a client, have them find the patterns or images.) Write them down. Describe what the images are. Imagine what the dreamspirits of the images want. Link the three images together in a story and observe what the story suggests about movement or lack of movement. Ask what these images might tell you about your question. Ask what else the images might tell you about your question. Pay attention to your own body as you tell these new stories. Which one resonates or feels right in your body, as opposed to just matching your current understanding? When in doubt, return to the object and the images.

I am always more comfortable helping people with their questions when I have something to read. A dream, an experience, an arrangement of objects, even the swing of a pendulum helps me separate out my own projections. When I help someone read a dream or an object they have brought to me, I provide options. I may feel one story more strongly than another, but I share the possible stories. Sometimes a client may not like the places the images lead them. When there is resistance, I remind them that these are their images, I'm simply reading them energetically. They are free to choose the reading or reject it, but it comes from the images that have emerged from their unconscious—from their dream.

Double Signals

In Peru, the word *kawak* suggests a higher form of vision. It is the ability to see the patterns of the dreaming reality and the way they are manifesting in everyday reality. It is the ability to pick up what Arnold Mindell calls "double signals":

> *When you use your first attention, you focus on your "primary processes," your normal identity, and rarely develop the second attention necessary to focus upon "secondary processes," the dreamlike events that transpire, such as accidents, slips of the tongue, and synchronicities. Hence, these secondary processes continuously happen to you without your involvement. Yet people around you notice them. You emit them as double signals.*

These double signals are the process by which your soul or your unconscious communicates in relationships. We've all experienced the sudden awareness that we are being lied to. We know what it feels like to instinctively not trust someone. These experiences are usually the result of incongruous double signals. When what someone is saying does not align with how they are holding their body, where their gaze is directed, or the tone with which they are speaking, we feel the presence of double signals.

On the other hand, you have probably also experienced people at moments where their conscious and unconscious expressions were so aligned that you felt instant trust, affection, or even attraction. There is no judgment involved in the perception of double signals. In fact, we are more likely to send double signals because we are deeply confused, troubled, or conflicted than because we are trying to deceive. A woman in a loveless marriage says, "Of course I love my husband," while her body is crying out that she is suffocating. A man overwhelmed with responsibility says with confidence and bravado, "I can handle this new workload," when the constant presence of little crises around him tells a different story.

Reading the double signals people project and being aware of your own can help you better understand the field in which an event is occurring. (We will discuss the impact of field awareness in later chapters.) It can help you shift your consciousness to a point outside that field to access compassion or to move more deeply into that field in a way that moves energy rather than leaving it stuck and stagnant.

❖ STONE AGE WISDOM PRACTICE #9:
Kawak: A Healer's Vision

The best way to begin practicing kawak is to apply it to situations in which you are not emotionally invested. These can be casual conversations with friends or even strangers. Parties can be a great place to practice kawak. You can also practice kawak by observing people in restaurants and shopping malls.

Let's imagine a casual conversation with a friend. Begin by checking in with your own body. Find your steady state. This is how you are feeling before the conversation begins. If you have a headache or a sore shoulder before you begin, then it is less likely to be a usable signal for you, though the amplification of pain might indicate a double signal. What is your emotional steady state? Are you annoyed, agitated, sad, or angry? Just be aware of where you are.

Now begin listening to what your friend is saying. To practice true vision-shifting, you have to be aware of the words she is saying as well as the way she is saying them. Every detail matters. What is the cadence of her speech? How long are the pauses? Where do they come? Does she seem comfortable or uncomfortable with her story? Does this feel like a story that she has told a lot? Is it a living story or one that is old and tired? Does her voice catch? Does she have to cough, swallow hard, or clear her throat when she talks about certain things?

Also watch her body language. Is she sitting forward or slumped back? Is she tense or relaxed? Is she fidgeting or moving nervously? Is she pulling herself into a tight ball or expanding? Does she hold certain parts of the body? Does she sigh, yawn, or take deep breaths? Is her breathing even or irregular? Use the softened vision described in Stone Age Wisdom Practice #7 or the focused strong eye technique. See what happens when you focus your gaze at your friend's third eye (between the eyes and on the forehead) or heart. Does it cause her to shift her position?

Scan your own body. Are you having bodily reactions to the exchange? Are you getting images or visions that seem unrelated to the conversation? Be aware of the immediate environment. What noises are intruding on the conversation? Are there pieces of other conversations that keep distracting you? What events intrude on the exchange? Are you interrupted repeatedly? Are there things you can see that your friend cannot that seem odd or unusual? Are there natural cycles that are being ignored?

Practical Kawak

I once watched a therapist work with a woman in a group process in which she was made the center of attention. The therapist pushed harder and harder to uncover the true nature of the woman's issue while completely ignoring the fact that a tiny bird had flown in a window and become trapped in the room. In a panic, the bird flew into a window and was knocked unconscious. One of the group members attended to the bird by picking it up and holding it while gently blowing air into its beak, and then setting it on a ledge outside until it was able to fly away. This event, totally missed by the therapist in first-attention mode, spoke more clearly of the woman's sadness and frustration than the therapist had been able to uncover.

Once you begin looking for these kinds of signals, it will be as if you were seeing things with new eyes. Many little signals will add up to a different understanding of what the person means to express. At this point, you have two choices—you can shift your awareness to the eagle's overview perspective, if you are ready to understand the dynamics of the situation in a new way, or you can shift your awareness to that of the jaguar, to move with controlled abandon more deeply into the experience.

From the eagle's perspective, you might begin weaving the spoken words together with the unspoken messages to fashion a new story—a larger story than the one being told. For example, over lunch a woman tells you a story about another woman who is having an affair. She shares all the details, but as she tells it you notice things like the fact that she leans forward and seems most interested in your response when she talks about the consequences of the affair. She repeatedly says that she herself could never have an affair because of the children or her love for her husband, but she clears her throat each time she says it. Her foot bounces to some agitated inner rhythm. You find images of yourself having an affair (real or imagined) coming to mind. You experience a tightness in your stomach, as if you are tensing up to prepare to be punched. You notice that the waiter is an attractive young man and that your friend seems to shift her persona every time he is around, making herself seem more flirtatious or feminine.

Without using your second attention, you might still be aware of all these signals, but they would be occurring at an unconscious level. You might find yourself becoming angry or irritated or judgmental without knowing what was upsetting you. You would be acting within a field of which you were unaware. Moving up to the eagle's view, you might begin to weave a new story. Here is a woman on the verge of having an affair, even if she hasn't fully admitted it to herself yet. She wants to know if you would judge her for it. She is deeply conflicted because she does care about her children and she does want to be faithful to her husband, but she feels drawn to another man or to an experience she does not believe she can have in her marriage. Your tension, your waiting to be punched, might come from your own similar unexpressed feelings. It might come from your suspicions about your spouse. Her shifting personas with the waiter might mirror your own unconscious behavior, or it might reflect something you've seen in your spouse. It might be enough to be more fully aware of the issues at play, to understand that the universe dreamed this friend with this issue to help you see your own.

From the jaguar's perspective, however, there is another course of action. You can move into the field and embrace the discomfort of the experience. To begin with, you might subtly mirror or mimic your friend's posture and way of holding her body. How does sitting this way make you feel? What does it illuminate for you? Lean forward when she leans forward. Feel the way she is using her body to emphasize certain sentences or thoughts. Bounce your foot the way she bounces hers.

Stop the conversation and ask the kind of direct question that sometimes can bring something into consciousness. "Are you having an affair?" "Are you about to?" "Do you think I would judge you if you had an affair?" We don't usually ask questions like this because we don't feel we can ask questions based on what we are intuiting. We are also afraid of making ourselves or the other person uncomfortable. But questions like this can suddenly shift a conversation of double signals into one that is highly congruent, because the conscious mind is giving voice to the unconscious. As an experiment, try giving voice to what the double signals you are picking up are suggesting in the form of a question. Stay calm and detached from any expectation. Hold the person in your heart with compassion as you ask. Then pay attention to the strength of the reaction—not whether there is agreement or not, but what is the energetic quality of the reaction.

Pay attention to what images come up for you. Move into those images. Imagine making love to the young waiter. Imagine having an affair. By embracing those images it does not mean that you must act on them, simply that you must bring them forward from your unconscious. If you are telling your spouse that everything is fine but the double signal you are unconsciously sending is that you've given up on finding passion in your relationship, you will not only make your spouse neurotic, but you will doom any chance of actually finding passion in the relationship.

Whether you use kawak to move to the eagle's view or to the jaguar's, you have brought light into the darkness, you have shifted out of an energetically stuck or unconscious place. You are actually perceiving at a new level. Everything feels more alive, shimmering with possibility. As you get more comfortable doing this, try it in more diverse social situations. Try to understand the group dynamics of business meetings. Apply kawak to other situations in your life. Gradually begin to use kawak for the issues to which you are emotionally connected.

Before moving on, I should mention that applying this technique can have unexpected consequences. Your attention is a gift. When you are able to direct both first and second attentions to another person, it will be felt. That person may perceive you as being wiser, friendlier, more compassionate, or even more attractive. This can go to your head. We are not used to being paid attention to in this way. We usually have to act out or over-dramatize to get the attention we think we need. If more people seek you out for your developing ability to pay attention, you may need to choose how much energy you have to give. You also need to be aware of how much this reverse attention plays into your needs. Let kawak illuminate your own double signals, and don't forget that you need to be vigilant and self-aware in this process. Just as you learn to watch, remember that you are being watched.

Learn to Read the Signs

As a hunter, there will be times when there are few signs for you to follow and the choice of what you hunt will be limited. But there will also be times when the signs of prey will be so abundant that the choice of which path to follow will not be so clear. Once you have opened your eyes to the possibility of signs and communication from the unseen world, it is time to develop compassionate discrimination. This is the ability to be open to what a living, conscious universe is telling you without being overwhelmed or incapacitated by it. The shaman pays attention to everything and then tries to ignore it, allowing the things that return to consciousness, things that really want the shaman's attention, to rise to the surface. Without higher vision, the shaman identifies too strongly with the material world. Without compassionate discrimination, the shaman runs the risk of identifying too strongly with the nonmaterial world.

Simply put, it is compassionate discrimination that helps you know when a traffic sign is just a traffic sign. I once had a friend so devoted to spirit and magic that for her, everything was a sign. She justified every action and every choice by the signs she was receiving. If we were talking about a new project in front of an elevator and the doors opened immediately after we pushed the button, it was a sign that we should proceed with our plan. While this sensitivity to signs helped her feel connected and confident, it led to as many bad choices as good ones.

Higher guidance should be seen as just that—guidance. Guidance does not absolve us from the responsibility of the choices we make. We are not here just to follow the orders of spirit guides. Shamans of most cultures spend a lot of time distinguishing between helpful and unhelpful spirits or energies. They learn how to get the most from both kinds of spirit, but they do not blindly accept every hint of guidance. As we open up to spirit guidance, we must be as careful as we would on any big city street corner.

Dreaming and vision-shifting help us open up to the signs, spirits, and energies of a living universe, but they are often not enough in themselves to give us clear direction. For that we may need to move deeper into the Dreaming in a conscious and connected manner. Our Stone Age ancestors developed various technologies for altering our consciousness. Now that we have a sense of a living universe, it is time to explore the consciousness of that universe.

Stone Age Wisdom Principles

Principle #2: The Second Stone

Everything is conscious.

Everything has its own form of conscious awareness.

Primal Alignment: Acknowledge

We learn to be present.

We learn to enter into true dialogue with the unseen

forces around us.

We alter consciousness in ways that allow us to engage spirit.

The Dreamer's Questions:

What does it want?

What wants to happen?

Shamanic Practice:

Journeying

CHAPTER 5

Journeying: Communicating with Spirit

We human beings are so designed that when
properly trained, we can interact with anything
that has consciousness on whatever level.

Itzhak Bentov,
Stalking the Wild Pendulum:
On the Mechanics of Consciousness

VISION-SHIFTING IS A GOOD WAY of coming to experience, and therefore know, that the world is alive. But while vision-shifting may take one over the threshold into an animated world, accepting that that world is not only living (vibrating or energetically alive), but also conscious, requires a deeper shift in awareness. Our Stone Age ancestors, regardless of where they evolved, developed technologies for altering their consciousness. It seems as if the need to experience altered states of consciousness is as deep and as old as any need we have.

John White, cofounder of the Institute for Noetic Sciences, has coined the term Homo Noeticus to suggest the next phase of evolution on the planet. Homo Noeticus, he proposes, is characterized by a shift from self-centeredness to God-centeredness. If this is true, then perhaps evolution is more of a spiral than a straight line, for it seems that Homo Noeticus describes who we once were as well as who we might become. We once lived in a world animated by living spirit. We sought to be in alignment and in a reciprocal relationship with that spirit. We have always sought ways to know the unknowable, experience the unseen, and come face-to-face with spirit. Now it seems that perhaps we are trying to rediscover that way of being.

Remembering the lesson of the Second Stone, we know that everything is conscious. Through consciousness we communicate. With vision-shifting, we learn to stalk. By the technique known shamanically as "journeying" or "traveling," we learn to engage. We acknowledge the consciousness around us by asking, "What does it want?" Tom Cowan writes in his excellent book *Shamanism as a Spiritual Practice for Daily Life*, "Shamanism is the intentional effort to develop intimate and lasting relationships with personal helping spirits by consciously leaving ordinary reality and journeying into the nonordinary realms of the spirit world."

A woman is asked by her partner in class for help with an issue involving harmful patterns in her relationships. She agrees to "journey" with her partner, even though neither of them will physically leave the room. They lie down side-by-side. A low, insistent drumming begins. They breathe deeply, relaxing the muscles in their bodies. They begin a visualization process that takes them into a primal otherworld. They harness the power of imagination as a trigger to carry them through a portal into another realm of existence. The world they enter is structured by a cosmology, but it is also an expression of their own soul territory. On this side of the portal they appear to be still, deeply relaxed, almost asleep. Their brain waves approach the deep theta state of 7–4 Hz often associated with deep trance or meditative states. Their levels of immunoglobulin A are elevated, suggesting enhanced immune system function. On the other side of the portal, they may be flying, swimming, shifting from one animal form to another, doing battle, making love, exploring, dancing, or sitting in council, all in an attempt to find an answer to the question posed.

When they hear the callback signal, they will return to their physical bodies and share their experiences. The answer to the question may come in clear, precise language relayed from a spirit guide, or it may come in the form of a poem or riddle, or an image. The answer may also be embedded in the experience itself and may need to be "opened" using the same techniques we applied to dreams in chapter 3. More often than not there will be what I have come to call the "confirmation detail." It may be the most obscure detail, the thing one is tempted to discard and not share because it doesn't seem to fit, that will be significant. But there will almost always be some piece of information, not previously shared and statistically improbable as a guess, with which the one who journeys for a client will return. That little piece will confirm that the experience is far more than imagination at work.

This is the technique known as journeying or shamanic journeying. It is not spirit possession or mediumship. You do not lose consciousness, you alter the frequency of your consciousness with intention, compassion, and discipline. By journeying, the shaman steps off the edge of consciousness with controlled abandon. The shaman is both the hunter and the warrior in this dream reality. He is not a passive spectator or tourist. He searches, acts, placates, mediates, battles, rebalances, learns, and transforms.

My third meeting with my spirit guide, Gray Morning Bear, came through a journey similar to my first, except this time rather than shape-shift and travel in the middle world, I journeyed to the upper world. This is the place usually associated with teachers and healing wisdom.

I am at the base of the point of departure I know as the World Tree. I climb up into its limbs. It is an easy tree to climb and I soon find myself far up in its green embrace. I move still higher, until I enter the clouds. Now it is as if I am in a dense fog. I climb higher and higher until I break through into the light. I step off the topmost branches onto solid earth.

I call hawk, the animal spirit ally that usually guides me in the upper world, and ask to be taken to visit Gray Morning Bear. So far it seems as if my relationship to this spirit teacher has to do with my own role as a teacher more than my role as a healer or my own personal issues, so I have decided to journey to seek some guidance on teaching journeying.

One of the things I find among my students is that there is a range of experiences in journeying. Some people seem to experience it visually, as if they were seeing everything. Some people experience it as an auditory phenomenon, as if someone was narrating what they were experiencing. Still others experience the journey as neither a visual nor an auditory experience, but one they characterize as a kind of "knowing." While I do not rank any of these experiences as being superior to the others, I find that my students often do, feeling inadequate if their journeys have not met their expectations. So my journey, my question, was designed to address this and ask for guidance as a teacher.

Hawk took me to Gray Morning Bear easily. We flew together over an emerald green carpet of prairie grasses into rolling hills. I found him piling dead wood together over stones in preparation for a sweat lodge. He did not address me right away, and I did not speak, but instead helped him gather the wood for his fire. After some time spent in silent work he moved under the shade of one of the few trees, and I joined him. We spoke of small things and I waited for what felt like the right time to ask my question, but I did not need to speak it out loud, for he sensed why I was there.

"When you come to me, when you cross over from your place to mine, you call a great horse to ride. The strong legs of that horse pound the earth like a heartbeat. It is your heart. It is the heart of the world. You come because you are doing the work of the heart, the work of love. You come with compassion, and that compassion is a horse with strong legs. The drum is the back of that horse. It carries you, but you must be attentive or you will fall off. You cannot ride this horse without discipline. You ride with a full heart and with presence, but you must also have intention. Intention is the head of this horse. Intention takes you where you are going. This horse will not come for you unless the journey you have *to make is powered by heart, managed by discipline, and guided by intention."*

We talked of more things, but it was not long before I heard the callback sound and took leave of my spirit teacher. I traveled quickly with hawk back to the World Tree, descended to its base, and returned to my body.

Our desire to alter our state of consciousness goes back a very long way. If one reads the creation myths of almost every culture, one finds a time when we were in communication with the entire world around us—a time when our consciousness was not a separate bubble of our own but rather a sea of awareness within which we swam. Even the Judeo-Christian tradition describes a time when we were as one with the animals and plants around us and our existence was a timeless garden. The desire to alter our consciousness might be described as an ache to return to that state.

Sound, movement, breathwork, isolation, deprivation, pain, and the ingestion of plants have always been used to alter our consciousness. While these paths have a place in traditional shamanic practice, we will not address the extremes of exhaustion, isolation, deprivation, and pain, because they require more preparation, supervision, and cultural context than a book can provide. Still, we have excellent choices available to us. As mentioned before, there are a wide variety of methods for inducing visionary trance states. Stanislav Grof, a pioneer in the field of consciousness studies, developed a technique known as holtropic breathwork to replicate the altered states of consciousness he experienced under the effects of LSD in the early '60s, before it was illegal. This rhythmic and patterned breathing induced transformational trance states. Felicitas Goodman has done fascinating work with body postures held for extended periods of time as triggers for trance and spirit journeys. Her work, based on the postures found on sacred statues around the world, suggests that the postures of yoga may have had a shamanic root. Gabrielle Roth and others have experimented with dance rhythms to induce trancelike ecstatic states. Trance journeys can also be induced with visual stimuli, such as mandalas and yantras.

The most common method of inducing a shamanic journey is with sound. This is true around the world and it is true among urban contemporary practitioners. Even when other catalysts are present, such as plant spirits, dancing, or breathwork, sound is often used to weave together or modulate the experience. Ayahuasca shamans of the Amazon use repetitive whistling to guide and structure the experience for the client. The Mazatec *curanderos* of Mexico use percussive prayer and chants to guide participants safely through the mushroom ritual or *velada* (vigil).

The most common technique for inducing a shamanic journey with sound was developed by anthropologist Michael Harner. It is taught by Harner's organization, the Foundation for Shamanic Studies, and owes its development to the drumming techniques of northern Siberian shamans. It involves listening to live or taped drumming while lying in a darkened room. Shamanic practitioners visualize a geographical point of transition between the material and the spirit worlds. They see themselves passing through a hole into a long, dark tunnel through which they follow a light and emerge in the lower world. Or, they might visualize themselves climbing a ladder into the upper world.

I use drumming and rattling to journey most of the time, but I came to a formal understanding of the techniques involved later in life and had been making journeys on my own since childhood.

I had already discovered that sound was a good trigger for my inner journeys. I sometimes use drone sounds such as chanting, sitar, and didgeridoo to journey, and I have had interesting success with contemporary sonic technologies such as the HemiSync approach developed at the Monroe Institute in Virginia. This music, when listened to through headphones, sets up alternate frequencies that entrain the brain to theta wave states.

For those new to the process, however, I find that the drum and the rattle are highly effective. Rhythmic induction is safe, easy to learn, and can be practiced alone with minimal equipment. There are some excellent books on the technique of shamanic journeying listed in the "Resources" (see page 266). It is impossible to cover the topic adequately in one chapter, but I can review the tools you will need, give you a sense of the territory to be covered, describe the basic steps, encourage you to make an exploratory journey, and suggest some important early journeys you might want to make.

An Urban Shaman's Tools

What follows is a list of the bare essentials you'll need for journeying on your own.

Sound system. Live drumming is a powerful experience. If you have a friend or a drumming group who will drum for you, take advantage of it. I urge you to journey to live drumming or rattling as often as you can. If you are going to make journeying a regular practice, however, you will want to be able to journey any time you choose. For this I suggest acquiring a personal stereo system. This allows you to make your journeying a private process. Shamanic journey recordings are available on CD and on tape. Recordings on CD have the advantage of flexible programming and better sound, while a tape system has some advantages if you are going to move or dance while listening to the music. I have recently converted my drumming CDs to MP3 format so I can store them on a small MP3 player.

A drumming tape or CD. As I said above, live drumming is perhaps the ideal way to journey, but a prerecorded tape or CD is easier and more practical. The Foundation for Shamanic Studies produces excellent quality recordings (see "Resources," page 266), but you may also choose to record your own. If you are going to record your own tape, you will need a drum, rattle, or click sticks. The rhythm should be between 205 and 220 beats per minute. Time yourself for short bursts of ten seconds to figure out the right rhythm. You should hit about 18 beats in ten seconds. This is a strong, driving rhythm. Don't accent beats or vary the tempo or rhythm. You are working to entrain the brain's rhythms to this sound.

You will probably want at least a 15-minute recording to begin with, though some of the recent research indicates that the effect of entrainment begins after about 9 minutes and peaks at 15 minutes, so you might want to opt for longer sessions. At 15, 20, or 30 minutes, pause the drumming and strike the drum deliberately for seven beats. Repeat these seven beats three more times, then begin drumming as rapidly as you can for about a minute. Pause again and do another set of seven deliberate beats repeated four times. This process is called the callback, and it signals that the journey is over and allows you about 2 minutes to return.

Your shaman's traveling journal. You will want to record your journey immediately after you return. It helps to have a book in which you record all your journeys. You will be logging the details of your explorations and excavations. Some people keep separate books for night dreams and shamanic journeys, but my own preference is to keep them together. It's easier to see patterns, relationships, and synchronicities if all your journeys into the Dreaming are recorded together.

A blindfold, bandanna, or cloth. If you will be journeying in daylight and the room or space you're in can't be made dark, a bandanna across your eyes may be used to eliminate distractions. Some of my students use lavender-filled silk eye pillows to block out the light. I use an interesting invention called a Mindfold (available through the Foundation for Shamanic Studies Web site; see "Resources" on page 266). It is a stiff plastic blindfold with foam pads that hold the surface up off your eyes so that your eyes can actually be open while you wear it.

A blanket, mat, or cushion. You will be journeying while lying on your back on the floor. You should be comfortable enough to not be distracted from your journey, but not so comfortable that you fall asleep. You may want a cushion under your head and a mat or blanket beneath you. A pillow or rolled-up blanket beneath your knees relieves lower-back pressure. If it's cold enough to be distracting, you might want a blanket to pull over you while you journey, as well.

The Territory

I can't tell you what you will see when you journey, but I can give you a sense of where you are going. Shamanic cultures around the globe share a triple world cosmology. While some cultures divide the three worlds into more levels, they invariably acknowledge a lower world, a middle world, and an upper world. There is no correlation between the Christian concepts of heaven and hell and the upper and lower worlds. The spirit journey is probably the primary religious experience for the hunter-gatherer cultures that have descended from our Stone Age ancestors, so these worlds existed long before Christianity.

Descending to the lower world is a way to connect with the Animal Spirits and the Ancestral Dead. It is the place to recover lost souls, find lost power, and appease the Master or Mistress of the Animals and the Plant Spirits. It is a journey for guidance and solutions. It is especially useful for learning about and healing issues of the past. It is often connected with the feet and with the serpent's-eye view of things. Ascending to the upper world means communing with the Cloud Beings, the Thunder Beings, the Sun, the Moon, and the Stars. It is also a place of evolved spiritual teachers, of healing and balancing wisdom, and of restoration. It is concerned with future events, the ears, and with the eagle or condor's perspective. The middle-world journey is a way of traveling, following distant movements, healing and communicating over a great distance, and recovering lost items. It is the realm of the present and is reflected in the hands. The middle-world view is that of the jaguar. The middle world is seen as an energetic version of our own waking world.

In contemporary terms, the place you choose to journey to should be decided by the intention of your journey. If you are seeking power, it is best sought in the lower world. If you are seeking wisdom, journey to the upper world. If you are applying the technique of journeying to resolve a specific and practical waking world issue, to find something lost, or because you need to communicate something over a great distance, you might consider a middle-world journey.

Is journeying safe? I can say that journeying with auditory triggers like drumming is as safe as dreaming. Does that mean that it will always be pleasant and happy? Are your dreams always pleasant and happy?

The more deeply you are able to journey, the more real and potentially frightening the experiences you may encounter. In cultures that have a warrior mentality, the shaman is seen as a warrior and her journeys are often battles or contests with angry spirits. This experience is not so common in urban contemporary shamanic practice, but it can happen. For that reason, we never take the process of journeying lightly. We do it with a clear intention, an open heart, and a sense of discipline. We are not just along for the ride. We use ritual and ceremony to express our respect for the world of Spirit, and we develop relationships with animal spirit allies that guide us and offer us protection.

I believe that ceremony is important to shamanic journeying. All shamans engage in some ceremony prior to journeying. This ceremony will usually reflect the culture from which the shaman comes. It may have been handed down through several generations, but it is just as likely to have been modified or learned directly from Spirit. My rituals reflect my studies with native North American, Peruvian, and Mexican shamans; my study of various cultural traditions from around the world; and my experiences in nonordinary reality. As such, I usually feel that the specifics of the rituals are not meant to be passed on as though the power resides within the ritual itself. What I can offer are some guidelines.

Before journeying, cleanse and consecrate your space. You can do this by lighting a candle with clear intention, smudging with sacred herbs (sage, cedar, or copal smoke for cleansing; sweetgrass, cinnamon stick, or lavender for attracting positive energies), shaking a rattle, or ringing a clear bell. Consider honoring the seven directions: north, south, east, west, above, below, and within.

If you have power objects, use them to define your space. Personal power objects may be bought, found, or given to you as gifts. Objects you make yourself will have the most power, but found objects or gifts from others can also be strong carriers of spirit. Your own set of ritual and ceremonial objects might include rattles, drums, or other rhythm instruments. You may want to have personal artifacts of power for the corners of your journeying blanket. This defines your sacred traveling space and helps you throw a protective field around yourself.

Begin each journey with a prayer and a statement of your intention. Just as in dream focusing, it helps to have questions stated clearly in advance. As you begin your journey, you will call on protective spirits, guides, and mentors. When the journey is completed, you will thank these same entities. At the close of each session, gently return the power objects you use to their pouches and places. Ritual focuses both attention and intention. It matters less what the actual ceremony is; what counts is that there is some structured activity that focuses your mind on the task ahead. The value of using the same ritual is that it more quickly entrains your mind and focuses you for your journey.

You might be wondering if journeying isn't just a case of very active imagination. After all, a shamanic journey begins with your *imagining* a portal between worlds. The only way to answer that is to try it for yourself. I don't want you to trust me, I want you to trust your own experience. Journeying does begin with imagination, in the sense that your power to visualize internal images jumpstarts the process. But it is what happens on the journey itself that is the real surprise. It is true that sometimes you can feel like you are forcing images to come to you, but other times you will be amazed by what occurs spontaneously. I find that I am most often surprised by dialogue. When I engage a figure on a journey in dialogue, I often get a lengthy and detailed answer faster than I could personally think up an answer in ordinary reality. I am also impressed by the fact that when I journey for someone else, there are always confirming details that I receive that have special significance to that person.

Our first journey experience will be a hybrid of a visualization and an actual journey. I find this is a good way for beginners to start because it offers guidance up to a point and then allows the journey process to take over.

◈ STONE AGE WISDOM PRACTICE #10:
The Sanctuary Garden Journey

The Sanctuary Garden Journey is a way of creating an inner sanctuary. It is a place to rest and renew your energy. It is a place that is peaceful and soothing. It has the capacity to relax and rejuvenate you, leaving you with more energy than when you started. When I was a high school teacher, I taught this technique to my students. They referred to it as a psychic field trip. Often my students reported that 15 minutes in quiet relaxation in their own Sanctuary Garden kept cold and flu symptoms under control for the day. My students also discovered that after retreating to their Sanctuary Gardens, issues seemed more manageable and conflicts seemed not so intractable. Your Sanctuary Garden will be your own private oasis of tranquility, safety, and personal healing.

Read these instructions all the way through before attempting the journey. Make sure that you understand your task clearly. Finding your Sanctuary Garden is a prelude to journeying to the

lower, middle, or upper worlds. In addition to being your sanctuary, your Sanctuary Garden may be the place you travel to first to
find your portals to the different worlds. On this first journey,
your intention will be to find or create your secret garden.

Put on a drumming tape or CD, lower the lights or slip on
your blindfold, and lie on your back on the floor with your arms
and legs uncrossed. Cover yourself with a blanket if you think
you'll become chilled. Pay attention to your breath. Take long,
slow, deep breaths from your belly. Begin to gradually relax your
body. With each exhalation feel the tension in your toes, feet, legs,
belly, hips, chest, arms, hands, fingers, shoulders, neck, face, and
scalp being washed away. Resist the temptation to fidget.

Begin to imagine a tall stone or brick wall. Is it covered with
ivy or hidden among tall trees? Does it emerge from a cliff, boul-
der, or hillside, or does it sit by itself? Walk along the wall until
you find a door or gate. This is your garden, and you will find a
way inside. When you find the door, push it open. Does it require
a key? If so, you will find the proper key in your pocket. Step
across the threshold. What is before you is the most relaxing environment you can imagine. It might be a flower-filled country garden with arbors and trellises and well-defined paths. It might be
a wooded setting filled with herbs and leafy green plants. It might
be a mountain garden filled with large stones, wildflowers, and
beautiful vistas. Look around for water. It may be obvious—an
ocean, lake, river, stream, or pond—or it may be a well, fountain,
or pool. Also look around for a shelter and a place to sit or lie
down. This may be a gazebo, a cottage, a cave, a cabana, or a
chapel. Pay attention to what you see.

Now, what would you like to see? You can imagine into place
anything you can see clearly. You might add crystals, furniture,

sculptures, specific plants, or personal items. What sounds would you like to hear? How about wind chimes or running water? How about bird song or a soft flute? Are there animals around? If so, they will not be threatening. They will be animals that support your growth and the work your soul is committed to. Remember that you can delete or un-imagine anything you don't like.

Spend some time in your Sanctuary Garden. Wander around. How big is your garden? Does the wall extend all the way around it? Investigate the shelter you created. The items you find in the shelter are your things. If they seem unfamiliar, get used to them. Pick them up and hold them. Feel their weight and texture. Without *needing* to know the answer at this time, you might ask why *these* things have shown up in your garden.

Try changing the weather in your garden. Make the sun come out or go away. Try it misty and gray, warmly lit with late-afternoon sun, or cool and dew-covered just after dawn. See what your garden looks like at night under a full moon. Are there smells in your garden? What are they? Try sitting or lying down. What are the most comfortable spots within this space?

When you hear the callback drumbeat, look around for a small object from your garden that seems like a replica of an object in your walking life. Remember it. Also, rearrange something in a way you will remember, so that when you return to the garden you will connect with the last time you visited. Exit the garden and pull the gate shut behind you. Lock the gate behind you, if necessary.

Slowly return your conscious awareness to your body. Move your fingers and toes. Roll onto your side, and then move slowly into a seated position. Record your journey experience in your journal. Draw a plan or map of your garden (at least as much as you've explored). Do whatever you can to make the place feel real. Pay attention to how *you* feel. You should feel refreshed and recharged. You should feel calmer and have better energy. Find the object that you saw a replica of in your garden. Keep it with your sacred objects—it is a waking-world connection to this particular altered state of consciousness. If you can't find it, look for an object that bridges this dream experience with the waking world. If you find a photograph that approximates the look of your garden or the feel of it, cut it out and save it in your journal.

Your Sanctuary Garden is a place you can visit as often as you'd like. It might be the jumping-off point for all your journeys, or it might be a quiet refuge. Instead of a power nap in the middle of the day, spend 15 minutes in quiet meditation in your garden. Return to the garden as a break during periods of intense work. Use the garden to take time out from an argument or stressful situation. Teach the technique to the children in your life. This simple practice has real and measurable physiological effects. As you practice this journey, your breathing deepens and more oxygen reaches your brain. Your heartbeat and pulse rate slow. Your body shuts off the secretion of adrenaline and other stress-response hormones, while at the same time triggering the release of pleasure-producing endorphins.

With time and practice you will be able to access this place without listening to drumming. Simply closing your eyes, breathing deeply, and visualizing will be enough to trigger your return. As you return again and again to your garden sanctuary, pay attention to what is different. What has been moved or rearranged? Attending to the patterns you discover can be as revealing as working with your dreams.

I think it is useful for urban practitioners to begin journey-work with the kind of hybrid we just experienced. As a spiritual practice, this kind of sanctuary journey helps you master your states of awareness and functions as a kind of meditative practice. It also develops your ability to experience altered states of consciousness. Traditionally, however, the practice of guided visualization is not the same as a shamanic journey. Something different but difficult to describe happens when we move into the true shamanic journey. It is less predictable, more fluid, and more real, without necessarily being realistic.

In the next exercise you will experience a more freeform and authentic shamanic journey. This will be a lower-world journey, and the first thing you will need to establish is a portal. Lower-world journeys begin with a kind of descent through a hole or passageway down into the Earth. You might visualize a cave, a hole in a hollow tree, a crack in the Earth, a spring or lake, or any opening that calls to you. It helps if this is an opening you've actually seen because it will be easier to recall. It can be any size, because you will be able to shrink yourself down to whatever size you need to be. If you don't already have a location in mind, consider finding one by trying one of the following options.

• Take a long walk in the woods or a park. Move more slowly than you normally would, as if you were stalking something. Use the Vision Walk (see page 107) technique from the previous chapter. Look for hollow trees or holes that lead into the ground. Look for caves or overhanging rock formations. Find an opening that calls to you.

• Look through a travel magazine that has lots of beautiful photographs of different places. See if you can find an image of your opening.

• If you've kept dream journals in the past, reread them and see if something you've recorded calls to you. You might have already dreamed about your opening into the lower world.

• Before falling asleep at night, ask for a dream about a passage into the lower world.

Once you have your passageway, find a comfortable position and close your eyes. Imagine the opening you've chosen. See it in as much detail as possible. Imagine yourself crossing the threshold and moving through the opening. On the other side of the opening is a dark tunnel. It may be very dark at first, or it may be dimly lit. Visualize the details of the tunnel. If you can't see anything, feel the walls. Sense what the tunnel is like. Is it cool or warm? Moist or dry? Experience the tunnel, but don't proceed any further. After familiarizing yourself with the tunnel, see yourself turning around and exiting through your opening.

Visualization is an important trigger for this experience. It's important that you clearly imagine as much of this as you can. You will find that when you do this with the drumming, the experience will take over and you will find yourself not so much imagining as experiencing.

When you are ready to try an exploratory journey into the lower world with drumming, return through your opening to the tunnel you imagined. Proceed down this tunnel. It will be dark at first, but with discipline you will see a faint light. Follow this light to the end of the tunnel. What you see at the other end of the tunnel will be the shamanic lower world for you. I could describe what *I* see, but it will not be the same for you. This is your world to explore.

Remember that it's also possible that you won't *see* anything. Not all shamanic practitioners experience this process visually. You may hear your journey, as if it were being described simultaneously with its occurrence. You may just know what happens. Your experience of the Dreaming may be misty and vague in the visual sense, but you will be certain of what occurs and whom you meet. Your journey may be a visual experience, an aural experience, a kinesthetic or somatic experience, or some combination of these. You can have rich and successful journeys regardless of which shamanic sense you favor.

◈ STONE AGE WISDOM PRACTICE #11:

The Lower-World Journey—Tracking Soul Blocks

Your intention for this journey is to visit and explore the lower world to discover what is keeping you from achieving a particular goal. This is the process of tracking soul blocks or energetic blockages in your life. You do this again and again for yourself and possibly for others. Don't feel that you have to answer all life's big questions on this first journey.

Take a few minutes to think about a goal that is currently eluding you. Your first response may be that no goal is eluding you and nothing is missing or out of balance in your life, but chances are that there *is* something you want to work on. After all, the feeling that something is missing or out of balance in your life probably prompted you to pick up this book in the first place. Phrase your question as openly as you can. Be more specific than "Why am I unhappy?" Don't set up questions for yes or no answers. Instead of asking, "Should I take a particular job offer?" try asking, "Which job will best serve the needs of my soul?" Instead of asking, "Which choice should I make?" ask, "What do I need to know to make the best choice?" Write this question in your journal along with the date at the top of a blank page. Remember that your question is your intention, and it will direct your journey. Remember also that compassion for yourself is essential. For the best answer, try to detach from the outcome.

Set your journey for a time when you won't be disturbed. Turn off your phones, draw the curtains to darken the room, and make sure that pets won't disturb you. Make yourself comfortable by lying on the floor with your arms and legs uncrossed. Put a bandanna or cloth over your eyes if the room is not fairly dark. Put your headphones on if you're using a personal sound system, and have the controls within easy reach.

As you did with the Sanctuary Garden journey, pay attention to your breath. Take long, slow, deep breaths from your belly. Begin to gradually relax your body. With each exhalation, feel the tension in your toes, feet, legs, belly, hips, chest, arms, hands, fingers, shoulders, neck, face, and scalp being washed away. Resist the temptation to fidget. As you breathe and relax, repeat the question that is your guiding intention for this journey.

As the drumming begins, visualize your opening. See it in all the detail you can. Pass through your opening into the tunnel. Find the light and follow it. Even if it isn't clear or distinct, it will be there. Follow the light until you reach the other side of the tunnel. If you don't see the light right away, walk forward for a while and it will appear. If for some reason the tunnel becomes blocked, find an alternate route. There will be another way. This tunnel is not designed to defeat you. Follow the light to the end of the tunnel. It's important to remember that when you go down into the tunnel, you are not literally going into the Earth, you are passing through an opening into another world. When you reach the source of the light, you will be through the portal into the lower world.

You will find yourself in a landscape. Explore this landscape. Get to know it well. It will be country you pass through again and again on future journeys. Look around and pay attention to details. Think about how you might map this location. If you see animals or people, make note of them. If an animal or person addresses you, you may choose to engage in conversation. Ask questions about this world. Ask to be shown around, but try not to stray too far from the opening to your tunnel.

This can be fun and intoxicating. Enjoy it for a while, but remember your intention. Use it to guide you to where you need to go. Remember that you may meet mentorlike figures or animals that you can talk with. Try asking them your question. They may answer you in plain, simple language. They may show you a scene or transport you to a place. Pay attention to this. They may hand you an object or perform some odd action to you or around you, or they may do nothing at all. Don't waste time if you aren't getting help. Move on.

When you hear the drumming callback, express gratitude for what you've received. Take your leave of anyone you are talking with, politely; you may need their help again. Return to your tunnel and follow your route back to your personal passageway.

Come back from your journey slowly. Move your consciousness back into your body. Reorient yourself. Remember what you saw as clearly and as completely as you can before you open your eyes. When you're ready, open your eyes and log your journey in your journal. Sketch what you remember. Diagram or map your route. These activities make the experience more real and more familiar. If you accept what you've seen or experienced as manifestations of Spirit or divine guidance, that's fine, but at this point it isn't necessary that you accept anything. For now, it's enough to make a record.

The dreaming world of the shamanic journey is the same reality as the world of our night dreams. It's filtered differently because we have maintained between 1 and 10 percent of conscious control over the experience. This awareness that maintains consciousness allows us to ask questions directly and to be shown or told, or even read, the answers to our questions. It is like becoming lucid within our dreams.

The return from a shamanic journey sometimes requires less unfolding of metaphors and deciphering of meaning than a nighttime dream does. You might have a clear idea of which job will best serve the needs of your soul. A dreamspirit within the journey might have told you specifically. However, there might also be things that need to be deciphered. Here are some of my students' experiences tracking soul blocks, and how they were interpreted.

• A woman swims underwater with salmon as an animal ally. She swims and swims in a way that seems pointless and boring, and when she is about to complain a disembodied hand draws a yellow band of light from one side of her rib cage to the other across her solar plexus. The salmon speaks to her and tells her, "You've just got to let go." After the journey she connects the solar plexus area with the chakra of the same name. This area is considered to be the seat of the personality—our sense of our personal history and who we are. The message seemed to be that she needed to let go of her tightly held sense of her personal history to make room for new possible stories in her life.

• A man worried about what was interfering with his promotion at work experienced a wild journey in which he found himself desperately trying to keep a series of holes filled with water. Before he could fill his fourth hole, the first would need water again. Blackbirds were cawing wildly as he worked. Finally a tiger grabbed him by the arm and held him by the first hole. He was able to successfully keep that hole filled with water as long as the tiger kept him trapped. After the journey he had the break-through realization that he did so many things at work that no one associated him with any one success. He decided to narrow his focus to starting and finishing a smaller number of projects on which he would stake his reputation.

• A woman potter with an artistic block meets an old woman who takes her back to when she was young and used to make pots out of clay she scooped from the riverbanks near her childhood home. She realizes in the journey that her sense of magic and wonder about her art form had faded away and that she needed to recapture her childlike enthusiasm for working with clay.

Lower-world journeys are extremely useful for our personal soul work. They can help us stalk and integrate our own power and eliminate energetic blocks. They tend to best address issues of physical and emotional healing. The difference between lower-world journeys and upper-world journeys can at times be subtle. Upper-world journeys tend to be about our spirit work. The upper world is a good place to go to get the eagle's-eye view of a conflict or situation. If I'm concerned with my own issues in a situation, I might make a lower-world journey. If I needed to find a solution for a business, family, or community—one that required an understanding of the field dynamics being acted out—I might choose an upper-world journey. The upper world is a good place to find wise mentors, teachers, and spirit guides; to seek vision and clarity; and to work on the future.

As for the terrain, my own experience is that lower-world journeys are very earthy and physical. They tend toward sensual and primal imagery. My journeys into the upper world move toward light and pattern and abstraction. Beyond this personal sense that I've shared, the best way for you to understand the difference is to experience it yourself.

As with the lower-world journey, you begin an upper-world journey by visualizing a point of departure. The shamans of Siberia visualize themselves rising up on the smoke of a fire through the smoke hole in a tent. Another popular method of ascent is a World Tree. This mythic tree straddles the lower, middle, and upper worlds. By descending down through its roots, one accesses the lower world. By climbing high into its branches, one enters the upper world. Some shamans imagine ascending mountains or climbing ladders, ropes, or vines up into the sky. Still others imagine themselves carried on the backs of birds, climbing a rainbow, or riding a tornado. I suggest using a tree, a tall ladder, or a tower with stairs that lead up. If you have a fear of heights, the tower might work better than the ladder. If this is someplace you've actually been, so much the better.

As I mentioned earlier, it is possible to link your points of descent and your points of ascent together in your secret garden. I have grown used to a tree with a hole at its base through which I can descend into the lower world. I use the same tree's branches to ascend to the upper world.

The Upper-World Journey—Planting a Soul Seed

Your intention for this journey is to visit and explore the upper world to set an intention for the future in the form of a Soul Seed. A Soul Seed is an idea about your future that you are choosing to set into motion. The upper world has the most influence on your future, so it is an ideal place to seek visions of your future and to set your intentions.

Let's imagine that a lower-world journey helped you clarify a personal story from the past that was limiting you in the present. A man I worked with found himself locked into a familiar story for men in this culture—the story of the warrior. It might have been a story that served him well in the past. It might have helped him find the energy to do amazing things. But now that story was not serving him so well. He had achieved success piled upon success, one victory after another, and still he felt empty. He had stayed too long and too rigidly in the warrior mode, and he had sacrificed most of the intimate relationships in his life.

His lower-world journey had been a kind of nightmare in which his armor was torn away, melted down, and reforged into a beggar's bowl. But he came through the experience stronger, resolved to make a change. Planting a Soul Seed was just the thing he needed to do. In this case, his Soul Seed was the intention to find a better story—perhaps a story of alliance, rather than combat. He set the intention to work on finding win-win situations where he once only saw win-lose struggles.

Take a moment to think about an intention you would like to set for the future. Be clear about what you are asking for. If you are seeking change, are you really prepared for the change you might receive? Have you thought about how it might affect you and those around you? Just because it affects people around is not a reason to avoid it, but you should be prepared for the possible reactions.

Write your intention on a small piece of paper and fold or ball it up like a little seed. Hold this seed in your right hand as you journey. As before, set your journey for a time when you won't be disturbed. Make yourself comfortable by lying on the floor with your arms and legs uncrossed. Cover your eyes if the room is not fairly dark. Put your headphones on if you're using a personal sound system, and have the controls within easy reach. Take long, slow, deep breaths from your belly, and begin to gradually relax your body. As you breathe and relax, repeat the question that is your guiding intention for this journey.

As the drumming begins, visualize your method of ascent. See it clearly. Climb or ride upward. It will not be hard to climb; you may feel weightless. You may catch occasional glimpses of how high up you are, or you may pass up into cloud layers. Eventually you will have the sense of passing through an ethereal membrane. This is the opening to the upper world. Now you will be able to step off onto ground that will support you. At first the landscape may be misty, blurred, or out of focus, but as you move forward, things will come into focus. The upper world tends to be more fluid than the lower world, so don't be surprised if the landscape itself seems to transform before your eyes.

Explore this upper-world landscape. As with the exit to your lower world tunnel, this will be country you pass through again and again on future journeys. Look around and pay attention to details. You may see animals here, but you are much more likely to see human-looking spirits. You can ask for help, guidance, healing, or knowledge. If you develop a particularly positive relationship with a spirit guide, you might ask if you may return to continue learning.

One of the things you might ask is where the best place to plant your Soul Seed would be. You might also ask to see what it will look like as your Soul Seed sprouts and grows. Allow yourself to be transported to this place and imagine that you are digging a hole, turning over the soil, planting your seed, and watering it. When you hear the callback drum, return the way you came to reenter your body.

Lie still for a moment. Collect your thoughts. Remember as much detail as you can about your journey. Sit up or roll over and record your experience in your journal. Again, it is important to sketch, map, or diagram what you saw, heard, or felt. This activity deepens your connection to your experience. After you have finished, it's important to bridge this experience by actually planting your Soul Seed. Find a nice place, dig up a little soil, and bury your folded piece of paper. Instead of watering it, hold the intention and the image from your journey in your head, and blow this intention lightly into the Earth over your Soul Seed.

The man in the example above found himself in an upper-world desert, scraping a hole in the hard, cracked soil with his beggar's bowl to plant his Soul Seed. He then used the same bowl, forged from what had once been his armor, to carry water to the seed. As he sat providing shade for the seed with his own body, he understood something about the nature of sacrifice that had never occurred to him before. Before this, sacrifice had always meant "losing." Now he understood it as a completely different way of being that was beyond winning or losing. After the journey he not only planted his seed in the waking world, but he found a small hammered metal bowl that he kept on his desk at work as a visual reminder of the lesson of his journey.

The last journey we will explore in this chapter is a middle-world journey. The middle world is an energetic template for our own world, so it looks nearly identical to the waking world we experience every day, though it tends to shimmer more. The evidence of energetic movement is easier to see. A lost object might be invisible to the waking eye but might shine or call out to the shaman's strong eye. As mentioned earlier, most shamans interact with the middle world through vision-shifting. They don't need trance-inducing methods like plants or drums. They simply shift their way of seeing.

It is, of course, possible to make middle-world journeys, and sometimes a middle-world journey is exactly what is called for. When you need to find a lost item or check out a place before you arrive, do it through the middle world. When you need to check on someone who is miles away, you can journey there via the middle world. When you need to send energy to someone far off, a middle-world journey is called for. Middle-world journeys can also be used to energetically create community.

◈ STONE AGE WISDOM PRACTICE #13:
The Middle-World Journey—Healing Gifts
The easiest way to make this journey is to take some time to think about the circles in your life. By circles, I mean the groups of people to whom you are close and who are connected to each other. For instance, you might have an extended family circle of parents, grandparents, children, brothers, sisters, cousins, nieces, nephews, aunts, and uncles. How many people you include in this circle depends on how many people you would like to regularly check in on and send compassionate love and healing light to. You might also have a circle of friends from work that are important to you.

If you are a teacher, you might include a circle of students. If you are a healer, it might be a select group of patients or clients. You might have old and dear friends that you would like to include in this process, even if you haven't seen each other in some time. Organize these people into circles, and prepare for a journey just as you would if you were visiting the upper or lower worlds.

As the drumming starts and you begin to relax, imagine yourself rising up out of your body. Roll and float in the air. Turn to look back at yourself. You might notice a fine, infinitely elastic, blue-silver cord connecting your dreambody to your physical body. Continue to float up. Pass through the ceiling and roof and out into the sky. You can rise as quickly or slowly as you wish, but once you've done this several times you will want to move along quickly.

Pick a circle to start with, and imagine the place where one of the people in that circle lives. Almost instantly you will find yourself there. You will be able to see the person. Don't be overly concerned about whether you are seeing them as they actually are in that moment in the waking world. Sometimes you may see them just as they were at that moment and even be able to confirm that. Other times, whether they know they are being visited or not, their spirit bodies might appear to you in a different form, for the sake of privacy. Feel yourself channeling love and light through your luminous body. You needn't stay long. A simple touch, a whisper of affection and support, a kiss, or a healing breath can transmit a lot of energy.

While I have called this practice "healing gifts," I am not suggesting that this process itself can heal physical conditions. You may have every hope of healing someone who is ill, but this is not in your power to do without their consent or participation. What you are doing is giving them pure love and light energy to use in whatever way their spirit bodies decide. This is truly a healing gift, even if the outcome is not a cure or even an easing of symptoms.

As soon as you have visited one person, visualize the next. You will instantly be drawn to that person. As you become practiced at this, you will find yourself being whisked around a city, a state, or even a country. It can make you feel a bit giddy at times, but it will go quickly with its own rhythm. With some people, you will feel compelled to linger. With others, you will simply connect and move on. Even the socially well-connected can check in and share healing gifts with their circles in journeys of 15 minutes or less.

Once you have finished the circles, you can choose to return to your body even before the callback, or you can choose to direct your expanded capacity to channel light and love to some of the world's leaders, to some of the world's neediest people, or to areas or regions of conflict that need a calming influence.

There are many reasons to practice this exercise regularly. My more sensitive friends (those who have learned to trust their intuition) seem to know when I have "visited." This exercise also gives me a deeply satisfying feeling that reminds me of saying my prayers as a young child and remembering to include my family and friends. It is also a fundamentally shamanic task to take responsibility for weaving the web of community. Just don't be surprised when people you "visit" but haven't spoken to in a while call you up for a reason they can't even explain.

Our explorations of our Sanctuary Garden and our upper- and lower-world journeys have been for personal growth and development. Our middle-world journey transitioned us into the idea of journeying for others. While it is beyond the scope of this book to address journeying for others as a healer, it is important to realize that most shamans journey on behalf of others. It is easier to detach from the outcome when journeying for others. It is easier to separate out personal issues and desires when journeying for others. It also seems easier to stay on task and get a clear answer when journeying for others. But, having said all that, I still believe that there is value in learning to journey for ourselves.

When we journey for ourselves, we come to know our own soul and spirit territories. We learn that the universe is conscious and that we can communicate with the spirits and energies that are expressing themselves through us.

The more we listen to our dreams; attend to the living, animate, energetic world through vision-shifting; and engage that world as a conscious entity through journeying; the more we understand the lesson of the Third Stone—that the world is fluid, dynamic, and constantly changing.

Stone Age Wisdom Principles

Principle #3: The Third Stone

Everything is dynamic.

It is the nature of living things to move, change, and transform.

Primal Alignment: Sense Energetic Patterns

We learn to be flexible.

We develop a sense of when energy is moving and when it is blocked.

We learn to move energies not by mastering them but by merging with them.

The Dreamer's Questions:

Where is there movement?

Where is there blockage?

What is the precise point of conflict?

Shamanic Practice:

Shape-shifting

CHAPTER 6

Shape-Shifting: Dancing with Change

*Whereas many psychological and spiritual systems
propose explaining and avoiding blocks, shamans
claim that they contain "power" that only partly
belongs to you...Instead of fighting these forces
or trying to explain them, the shaman gives up
trying to change what he cannot grasp and
reorients himself by adapting to their direction.*

Arnold Mindell,
*The Shaman's Body:
A New Shamanism for Transforming
Health, Relationships, and the Community*

WITH AN UNDERSTANDING THAT THE universe is alive and conscious
can come a sense of anxiety. The universe, after all, is not a static
field. It is a dynamic sea that shifts and changes and totally transforms itself. Health is movement. Wholeness is expressed in our
physical bodies by the free flow of energy. Energies want to move.

It is their nature. We may not understand where they are going or what they want of us, but they will move. Denying or repressing movement creates blocks, and blocks are at best only temporary. Blocks make us sick and unhappy and require more and more of our personal energy to maintain. When the energy behind the block moves, it will move like water, seeking the path of least resistance. Try to hold water and it will slip through your fingers or splash over the edge of the container you've built. Try to block or restrict the movement of water, and pressure begins to build. Hold back the water long enough, and when it moves, it will wash away everything in its path. Interacting with a living, changing universe requires skills that we have never been taught. Our ancestors understood these skills. They called them shape-shifting.

We may associate shape-shifting with werewolf movies and the feats of mythical magicians, but shape-shifting is something we all do, whether consciously or not. When it is unconscious, it can be a defense or a way of avoiding claiming our own power. We camouflage ourselves to blend in with a group. We may unconsciously shift our speech and mannerisms around certain people. We may also shape-shift more consciously, as when we become the employee the boss wants us to be in order to get a raise or a promotion. We may consciously shift from one persona to another to sell, convince, or persuade. Neuro Linguistic Programming teaches a kind of conscious mirroring process to improve communication. Athletes and artists describe a feeling of losing their individual identities in the pursuit of a sport, hobby, or task that takes them out of themselves. The best surfer doesn't fight the wave, she becomes the wave.

Conscious shape-shifting can have practical applications in everyday experience. It can often be the only way out of otherwise intractable situations. Sometimes when we encounter others who feel the need to threaten and dominate us, it is because they are actually afraid of the world around them. They see others as threats and respond by striking first. Shape-shifting can be a way of altering someone's perception of you as a threat.

Michele Jamal records the observations of traditional Northwest shaman, Johnny Moses, in her book *Deerdancer: The Shapeshifter Archetype in Story and Trance:* "Traditional shapeshifting of today is used for successful strengthening of the mind. In order to understand someone's way of thinking, you must become that person."

Many years ago, as a teacher, I encountered an assistant principal with a reputation among teachers of being distant, hard, and difficult to work with. The other teachers in the school avoided her as if she were contagious, but they were at her mercy when she decided to show up in their classrooms. Being a new teacher and knowing that sooner or later she would be evaluating my teaching, I tried the technique of shape-shifting to find a way to be in balance with her. I began making a point of visiting her office at least once a day to study her. I noticed how precisely and carefully she dressed, how she organized her desk, and how she interacted with other people. It seemed to me that she had worked hard to move from being a teacher to an administrator, and part of her difficulty with teachers was that she needed so desperately to convince herself that she was not one of them anymore that she ended up alienating them. I also sensed that she was unhappy with this situation but was not conscious enough of the dynamics to change it.

I knew that playing the part of the subordinate teacher to her administrator would not work. I knew that some teachers had tried to ingratiate themselves with her in an artificial way and had failed miserably. I began to mirror some of her mannerisms in a very subtle way that would make her feel like I was someone she might be comfortable around. I would stop by, call her by her first name instead of her title, and otherwise treat her as a peer instead of a superior. I shape-shifted from being her subordinate to being her equal. Now, this could have easily backfired. It was her nature to be suspicious, and she would have picked up on the slightest bit of sarcasm or insincerity, so I shape-shifted with compassion and an open heart. I invited her to visit my class on a regular basis, always keeping her informed of what was going on in my class on particular days. I offered her information and established a relationship by asking her advice.

By the time she got around to formally evaluating me, she had been in my classroom many times by invitation. My evaluation became a friendly discussion between two professionals instead of the adversarial process I'd heard my colleagues describe.

I can't overstate the importance of heart in this process. While we never became great friends, I grew to respect and like this person. I changed in the process of shape-shifting. I did not limit myself to narrow and self-serving goals in the process. I opened up to the possibility of change, and I think that is what resonated with her more than any one superficial step I might have taken. This was not a rational process, but rather an instinctive and intuitive shape-shifting to alter her perception of who I was from a threat to a friend.

Conscious shape-shifting is a practical way to both understand and align with the dynamic nature of the universe. Through our dreams, our visions, and our journeys into the unseen, we begin to understand that the situations in which we find ourselves are often fields with clearly defined roles. We may have unconsciously been playing a role, allowing the dreamspirits of that field to express themselves through us. Being stuck in a field, a role, or a personal story means that we don't have the flexibility or the mobility we need to ever resolve the issues of that field. We have the same arguments with the same people again and again precisely because we are all stuck in energetic fields playing roles none of us is conscious of. We may try to avoid the person or the topic of contention by withdrawing from the field, but we can't really get out of it by explaining it or repressing it. What shamans and many martial arts teach us is that the opponent must be embraced. The force or energy must be engaged and redirected. It must not be blocked or restricted, but allowed to move in a way that harms neither opponent. To do this requires a merging, a melding with the other, a shape-shift.

Once, while sitting in ceremony with a small group, I watched a woman bring up an issue that had disturbed her. She had felt slighted and embarrassed by a man in the group, as if he had not been respectful of her right to be included in an earlier ceremony. She hesitantly but bravely shared her feelings, but I felt a sense of incongruence, an awareness that there were double signals being sent. The man listened patiently, then began to defend himself by explaining how the woman had misunderstood the situation and needed to be more respectful of the culture she was a guest of. Again, the argument sounded logical, but the feeling I had was that double signals were being sent again. The argument went back and forth and seemed to be growing more intractable. Under the guise of reason and logic, the man was working to convince the woman of the incorrectness of her feelings. At the same time, the woman was having difficulty expressing just what it was that she was upset about. The energy of the group was settling into a dark and heavy place. The "open" discussion was not helping, because it was not really open. Everything that was being said just pushed each person further into his or her role. At that moment, I had the strong feeling that Gray Morning Bear was sitting beside me. Though I could not see him, I could hear his voice.

"There are times when we need to fly," he whispered. "It will look different from above."

I shifted my consciousness outside of my body as I had been taught, and I found myself looking down at the circle. I realized in an instant that there was something deeper going on than anything that was being said. "You see the field now?" he asked.

"Yes, there is something here about the balance of masculine and feminine energy, but I don't understand it clearly. She seems to be speaking from the place of the wounded feminine."

"The spirit of the field is a wounded woman," he interrupted. "The spirit is speaking through her."

"And the man is speaking from his own wound, isn't he?"

"Yes," Gray Morning Bear answered. "But it is more like the wounded male spirit has chosen to speak through him because the man knows this wound so well."

"What should I do?"

"You need to show them the field."

"You mean tell them what I see?"

"Show them, don't tell them. You need to shape-shift. Feel the woman's pain and express it. Feel the man's pain and express it. Invite the dreamspirit to express itself through you."

"But don't I risk getting stuck in the field myself?" I asked.
"Take both sides and take neither side. Risk their anger,
and if they turn on you, laugh at yourself. Do the unexpect-
ed. Be ferocious or be a fool, but keep moving. Embrace their
roles so they are free to move to other roles or even free to see
the roles they were playing. Dance in the field. This is how
you move the energy and resolve the field."

I tentatively asked if we could pull back for a moment from the
process of explaining our positions. I spoke from the woman's
place, shifting my consciousness to align with what was actually
causing her pain (as opposed to what had triggered the field), and
I instantly felt the man's animosity toward me rise. I realized that
I must have successfully allowed the dreamspirit to move from
her to me, because now I was the focus of tension for the man.
Then I shifted again and expressed the pain I felt from the man.
Again, I tried to express the real pain as opposed to the
wounded pride. I felt the tension release from him, and because
the woman had been shifted out of her role for a moment, she was
able to hold that vantage point and not move back into it. The
energy began to move again. The resolution of the field did not
require apologies or group hugs or forgiveness. It required an
acknowledgement of the disavowed and repressed voices of the
dreamspirits of the field.

The art and practice of shape-shifting can best be understood as
occurring along a spectrum or continuum of mind, heart, and
body. My experience with the assistant principal began as mental
shape-shift and deepened into a heart-based or emotional shape-
shift. A shape-shift at the level of the body was not necessary, but

I believe that physical shape-shifting is not only possible, but that it, too, happens all the time.

For many years I had experimented with fasting as a means of altering my consciousness. I discovered quite by accident that after the first several days of a water fast, my energy level would dramatically increase and my need for sleep would decrease. I learned to use fasting to do extraordinary amounts of work in short periods of time. Often this work was the technical writing or creative projects that paid my bills, but the effect was still powerful.

One summer several years ago, I embarked on a fast with a spiritual intention that was different from my previous uses of fasting. I did not check into a spa or embark on a vision quest in some pristine wilderness, but rather dedicated a week to journeying, meditating, journaling, and exploring my connection to the unseen world. On the sixth night of my fast, I journeyed deep into the Dreaming. I ran with wolf, my power animal. I became a wolf. It was one of my most memorable journeys, but when I returned, I felt anxious, bubbling over with a raw energy. It was warm out, so I pulled on a pair of shorts and some running shoes and set out to run through my neighborhood.

Almost immediately I knew something was different. I could still feel the wolf within me. I had the sense memory of running as a wolf. My body began to shift into a different posture than I had ever experienced before. My spine arched, and I ran as if my hands were striking the ground, pulling me along, just as surely as were my feet. My mouth dropped open, and I began to pant. This was not the panting of someone out of breath, but a different way of breathing. The working of the left and right sides of my body slipped into a new rhythm.

The funny thing about it was that there was no trying on my

part—no will. I did not consciously set out to run like a wolf. I didn't try to mimic a wolf. If anything, I would say I surrendered to the wolf in that moment. Even writing about it now I can still feel the changes that I experienced that night.

But other things changed, as well. My sense of smell, which is usually my weakest or least-developed sense, came alive. I could smell the ocean and the brackish tidal pools, the remnants of meals cooked hours before in the houses I ran past, the simmering smell of garbage in cans beside the houses, the smells of animals and cars and perfumes. My eyes felt heavy, as if I was seeing through transparent eyelids, but the plants, the living things, glowed.

I have and had no "objective" way to gauge my experience, but I became aware of cats as I ran. I have cats and am used to how they react. I've run at night and passed cats many times before, but I'm convinced the cats saw me differently that night. They crouched, tense, eyes wide as I ran past. They had the wariness of urban cats when confronted with loose dogs. They froze, ready to run or fight in an instant. Some ran, others just studied me as a threat they could not categorize. (I should mention at this point that I did not wake up three hours later in a strange backyard with blood and cat fur sticking to my face.) I do not recall wanting to chase the cats or hurt them in any way, but I was certainly aware of them and they were aware of me.

I ran for two hours, and it felt like 20 minutes. I showered when I returned home and finally went to sleep. But even as I slept, I felt my body going through changes.

Was this shape-shifting? I believe that if it was not an example of shape-shifting, it was an experience along the continuum of experiences we call shape-shifting. I've had other experiences I would classify as falling along this continuum since then, but I mention this example because it did not occur in some exotic location or under the influence of plant spirit medicine. It occurred in an urban setting. Granted, there was ritual preparation, but there was no clear expectation or anticipation of shapeshifting. It was, instead, my ability to get out of my own way and surrender to the experience that allowed it to unfold. If I had been able to make the final step and lose the "observer" perspective over my experience, I'm convinced that the shape-shift would have occurred at an even deeper level.

The Shapeshifting Continuum

So what is shape-shifting? Shape-shifting, I believe, is a range of experiences that involve the intentional surrender of those things that keep us separate and distinct from the plants, animals, objects, and forces around us. When we accept that the universe is alive and conscious, it is because, at some level, we realize that we are all essentially made of the same stuff. John Perkins, in his book *Shapeshifting: Shamanic Techniques for Global and Personal Transformation,* describes a conversation about the practice of shape-shifting with the Mayan shaman Viejo Itza:

> "And you are also mistaken if you think they are merely taking on the appearance of something."
>
> "What then?"
>
> "They become this 'other.'"
>
> "How do they accomplish this?"
>
> He gave me a fatherly smile. "You know very well how they do it. They don't really become this other at all, because all along they were this other. They and it are the same."

Physics and contemporary science confirm this without being willing to fully acknowledge its implications. But this awareness is usually an intellectual knowing. It is seldom experienced as a bodily knowing. One way of thinking about shape-shifting is that it is the experience that brings the awareness of universal interconnectedness into the body.

Shape-shifting begins at the level of mind. When we study an animal or plant, observing it with patience and attentiveness, we are initiating a shape-shift. Many of the vision-shifting techniques shamans use (and some of the ones described in chapter 4) are actually the first step in a mental shape-shift. Before we can move our consciousness into another form, we have to imagine the possibility of shifting our consciousness outside of ourselves. One of the best ways to learn about shape-shifting is through an animal connection. Shamans around the world refer to power or medicine animals. These are animal spirit allies with which the shaman has a special bond and may, in fact, share a shape-shifting relationship.

When I teach this, I have students first connect with animals by studying their forms. I encourage them to surround themselves with images or figures of their particular animal. They may watch films of the animal. They may even be able to observe the actual animal in a zoo or the wild. We ask what the animals are in and of themselves, how they behave, and what makes them distinctive from other animals. At the level of mind we become familiar with our power animals, while maintaining the distinction between them and us. We allow a little of their archetypal energy to enter our energy fields, but we do not lose awareness of ourselves.

Moving along the shape-shifting continuum, we drop into the heart, or the realm of emotional knowing. At the heart level, we invite the animal spirit into our bodies. In a sense, we agree to share space. We may dance or move like an animal. We may breathe or make noises like an animal. We allow the archetypal energy of bear, puma, condor, or wolf to fill us. This mimicking of animal forms is characterized by sudden shifts in perception. One minute we are ourselves, the next moment we are the animal. We are both at the same time. When undergoing a shape-shift at the heart level, we might characterize the overall experience as being 50 percent us and 50 percent animal. But in the middle of the experience, we probably lose our sense of self in the animal completely in one moment and then have a hard time not thinking ourselves foolish the next moment.

It is important to understand that even though the mental and emotional levels of shape-shifting fall short of the dramatic kinds of effects we might associate with shape-shifting, they are each significant. We learn and are changed by our experiences. In my own experience, studying wolves at the mental level taught me about a social organization that gave me a useful way of thinking about my relationship to others in my life. I have always been torn between a need for social contact and a need to be alone. Wolves live this reality, functioning for long periods of time as members of a pack and yet also capable of walking away from the pack to spend long periods of time in solitude. From this model, I learned that I might manage to meet both needs in my life, and that I did not need to pick one way of being at the expense of the other. This was a mental shape-shift. By allowing myself to be filled with the spirit of the wolf at the heart level, I developed a deep compassion for wolves and how they exist. I brought my struggles with the social versus the private into alignment with wolf energy and found some peace. I did not return from either of these shape-shifting experiences unchanged. I was somehow different for the experiences I'd had.

In this continuum of shape-shifting, the final level is at the level of the body. This is the cellular shape-shift—the shape-shift that brings true physiological transformation. Think of the transformations you've seen in every werewolf movie or the physical shape-shift experienced by William Hurt's character in the film *Altered States*.

Shape-shifting at the bodily level does happen. At a purely physical level, every time we inhale and exhale, we are shape-shifting—exchanging molecules and atoms and becoming something new. If medicine can record instances of cancers and tumors disappearing from the body, why would it seem strange to think that skin or hair or bone tissue might alter? Indeed, many people have witnessed shamans transforming into pumas, condors, and pythons. Instances of bodily shape-shifting may be as dramatic as shamans who appear human one minute and the next minute are replaced by some animal, or shamans who grow tufts of hair, alter their skin surface, or manifest bone deformities.

Shape-shifting at the level of the body is the most difficult of transformations precisely because it is the most frightening. At the level of mind, we discretely sample some animal energy. At the level of heart, we share body space with animal energy in a duality or split perspective. At the level of body, we lose our human frame of reference. We become the animal or the animal becomes us. This is frightening because we need to be willing to let go of our ego consciousness to bring the shape-shift into the body, and, once we do that, we know that we may not find our way back. For this reason, shape-shifting is not a practice for those with a weak self-image. Shape-shifting at the bodily level is, paradoxically, an act that requires both great personal power and the ability to abandon any attachment to that power.

As with the other levels of shape-shifting, bodily shape-shifts change us. They may heal us or transform us in real, verifiable ways, or we may simply pick up a new physical skill. When I shape-shift into the wolf at the bodily level, I might discover a way of running that feels like the effortless loping of a wolf crossing a snow-covered plain.

I describe this process as a continuum because no single instance of shape-shifting fits neatly in one category. The shaman studying an animal at the level of mind may be drawn closer to what looks like heart-level shape-shifting. My experience of running as the wolf was a heart-level experience that slipped, I believe, into a body-level shape-shift.

I don't mean to imply a hierarchy here. One form of shape-shifting is not superior to another. We can learn important lessons from experiences all along the shape-shifting continuum. And, while I'm sure there are exceptions, it may be that we cannot just jump to the bodily level of shape-shifting. We may need to work our way through mind and heart first.

If we think of shape-shifting as growing out of primeval hunting and gathering practices, we can see the model more clearly. The young hunter or gatherer grows up studying the plants or animals he or she will be seeking. Patterns are learned, habits memorized, forms identified. Next, through ceremony, especially in the case of the hunter, the animal spirit is called down. The hunter embodies the animal, often dressing in skins, wearing antlers or bone fetishes, and covering himself in the scent of the animal. On the hunt itself, the hunter may actually lose himself to better hunt his prey. The shaman may become the eagle to fly out in search of the herd, or he may become the bison mock-sacrificing himself in ritual for the sake of the hunters.

The shape-shifting continuum tells us something about change and transformation. It might also have implications for healing. If transformation needs to drop from the level of mind to the level of heart before reaching the level of body, perhaps healing needs to follow the same path. We've all heard the "New Age" mantra that we are responsible for our own illnesses and our own health, as if awareness of this fact ought to somehow be enough to transform the situation. Unfortunately, even when we know this and accept it on the mental level, we may not experience any healing transformation. This in turn adds to our own sense of guilt and responsibility for our illness, just making it worse. Perhaps what we need to do is acknowledge the possibility that we have contributed to our condition and have the power to reverse it at the mental level—perhaps by exploring it with a therapist, spiritual counselor, or friend. Then we might need to drop that idea down to the level of the heart by making art or practicing ceremony. By becoming a representation of the illness, we begin to be able to shift it from the inside.

John Perkins speaks insightfully about his initial fascination with the "trick" of shape-shifting. But the more he pursued the "trick," the more shape-shifting became something much greater. Shape-shifting came to be a model for change.

If I want to change the world, the best place (and perhaps the only place) I can start is with myself. I can study that thing I want to change, accepting the possibility of change and setting the intention to change at the mental level. Then I can enact the change. This might be the famous "fake it 'til you make it" rule. I can act as if it has changed. I can begin to embody the change. Finally, once that emotional level has been reached, once I feel the change, it becomes second nature to me. I no longer "think" about it. Now I free myself from attachment to outcome as I drop the change into my bodily awareness. At this level, there is nothing left to change and no distinction between the thing needing changing and the person making the change. To paraphrase a famous bumper sticker: "Change Happens!"

The shape-shifting model of change works at the individual as well as the communal or institutional level. At the communal or institutional level, another dynamic enters into the continuum: critical mass. As Rupert Sheldrake has described in his theory of morphic resonance, change isn't dependent on unanimous consent but rather on critical mass. When enough people (or animals) adopt a new way of doing something, it somehow enters the culture with a force that is disproportionate to the actual number of people (or animals) practicing that new adaptation. So, it would seem to follow that a small number of institutional or communal shape-shifters could have a disproportionate effect on planetary change. I would take this one step further and posit that the force of 100 people shape-shifting at the bodily level is equal to roughly 1,000 people shape-shifting at the emotional level, which is equivalent to 10,000 people shape-shifting at the mental level. Again, there is no implied hierarchy here. Planetary change can effectively utilize shape-shifters at all levels.

In the end, shape-shifting is a skill that is worth attending to. We learn as we shape-shift. We can heal and transform when we shape-shift. While we may not all fly as the eagle, we can invite the flight of the eagle into our hearts.

Finding Your Power Animal

One of the most useful allies you can have in your practice of Stone Age Wisdom is a power animal. A power animal is an animal with which you have a deep and intimate connection. Your power animal is a guide, confidant, protector, teacher, and shape-shifting double. Your power animal is a spirit manifestation of your power. You connect to a particular power animal because there is a resonance between what your soul needs or what your soul mission is and the particular wisdom of that animal. Though I know some of my fellow practitioners will disagree, I think that we really only have one power animal at a time. We may have many animal allies. We may have old power animals that remain with us as allies even when a new power animal shows up, but that is not the same thing as a power animal. Even if one feels that he or she has many power animals, it is most useful to deeply explore the connection with one animal for several years.

Power animals are not the Beanie Babies of the spirit world. I know some people who collect them as if the materialism of the physical realm has invaded the spirit realm. Your power is not reflected in the number of power animals you have. I often tell my students to think of their power animals as a real presence in their lives. Consider whether caring for an actual lion, elephant, python, two wolves, and a wolverine would be a reasonable thing for you to fit into your schedule on a daily basis. Maybe you can support that many power animal relationships, but I doubt it. Shamans in traditional cultures spend a great deal of time cultivating their relationships with their spirit guides and power animals. Don't claim more than you can honor and care for. Take your power animal relationship seriously. Be reasonable and be respectful.

Acquiring a power animal is not as difficult as it might sound. You actually already have one. It may have wandered off because you weren't caring for it, or maybe you just haven't been introduced yet. In the Australian bush and the African veldt, people believe that when a child is born, a spirit animal comes into existence. It can take a physical form and if it dies or is killed mistakenly, it can have disastrous consequences for the person connected to it. This is why hunting is always a sacred act done with respect for the animals. If you are truly connected to your power animal, you will be filled with power. Being filled with power means that there is no room for spirit intrusions (the shamanic language for infections). It increases your physical energy and your ability to resist disease. If you have long felt a strong kinship with a particular animal, that may be your power animal. One way to untangle a romantic attachment to an animal from an actual power animal connection is by doing a power animal journey.

◈ STONE AGE WISDOM PRACTICE #14:

Lower-World Journey—Seeking a Power Animal

Your intention for this journey is to visit the lower world to meet and connect with your own power animal. Remember that, as with all journeys, you will need:

1. Clear intention—an intent to meet your power animal.
2. Compassion—a heartfelt desire to connect with the right animal, as opposed to the one to which you might be sentimentally attached.
3. Discipline—the perseverance to continue the process until the correct animal shows up.

Avoid alcohol or mind-altering substances for 24 hours. Fast or eat lightly during the day leading up to the journey. Arrange your journey for a time when you won't be disturbed. Make yourself comfortable by lying on the floor with your arms and legs uncrossed. Put a bandanna or cloth over your eyes. Start your drumming CD.

Take long, slow, deep breaths from your belly. Begin to gradually relax your body. Resist the temptation to fidget. As the drumming begins, visualize your opening to the lower world. See it in all the detail you can. Pass through your opening and into the tunnel. Find the light and follow it until you reach the other side of the tunnel.

Begin to explore the lower world in search of your power animal. You may see many animals, but your power animal will appear to you four different times. It may look slightly different each time. It may appear in living form twice, as a stone sculpture once, and as a picture once. All these forms are equally valid. Your power animal may be any kind of animal, bird, fish, reptile, or even insect. Don't let your prejudices keep you from learning the lessons of a particular power animal. Some people recommend that you avoid animals that repeatedly bare their teeth or fangs at you. I think this makes good common sense, but don't avoid animals that simply open their mouths. If you feel you are being threatened, this is probably not your power animal, anyway.

When you have seen the animal four times, clasp it to your heart with both hands. This should not be a struggle because your power animal should want to come willingly. Once you have the animal in your heart, return quickly through the tunnel. Try not to lose your power animal in the process. When you have returned to your body, feel your power animal spirit expand from your heart to fill your body. Slowly roll onto your side and begin to move like your power animal. Move into the posture of your animal, then begin to dance as your power animal.

Later, find images of your power animal for your journal. Find representations of your power animal for your altar, or wear a charm that symbolizes your relationship to it. Honor your power animal by creating an altar dedicated to it and checking in at that altar on a daily basis. Create a medicine bag for your power animal. Get a small leather pouch and begin to fill it with items that bridge the journey experience with the waking world and connect you to your animal. Your pouch might contain a fetish sculpture of your animal, fur, claws, bones or other parts of that animal, some symbolic food for your animal, or an image of that animal painted on stone or wood. There is no wrong way to create a medicine pouch, just don't make it so big or heavy that you can't easily travel with it or keep it near you.

Learn about the characteristics of your power animal. We often rush to learn the "meaning" of an animal according to one native tradition or another. While this may be interesting, it is also disempowering. The meanings associated with animals did not spring out of nowhere. They grew from hundreds of thousands of years of close observation and intimate relationships. Give yourself the chance to learn about your animal before adopting a cultural "position" on it. Before consulting dream dictionaries and guides that suggest the cultural associations with specific animals, learn about the actual animal behavior. Check out Animal Planet or the Discovery Channel before using a dictionary of the symbolic meaning of animals. What we want to know is how the animal behaves in the wild. What are its characteristics?

One woman learned from her research that salmon undergo a complete physical transformation in the process of returning to the place they came from. She also learned that only Pacific salmon return to their spawning grounds to die. Atlantic salmon make the journey to their spawning grounds over and over again. These facts had more personal meaning for her than the dictionary associations with salmon.

Honor your power animal on a regular basis. I suggest that students take a day every so often to do something their power animal would enjoy. This might mean taking a run in the woods for a wolf; eating a thick, juicy, rare steak for a grizzly bear; munching on a garden-fresh salad for a rabbit; or going for a swim in the ocean for a dolphin. Make journeys to the lower world specifically to commune with your power animal. Consider volunteering at a zoo or wildlife park or making a donation in support of the earthly, physical manifestations of your power animal.

Whenever you journey, call your power animal to you. Your power animal will make tracking, navigating, and traveling much easier. It will also serve to protect you and, if you wish, remove you from any situation that seems frightening or threatening. Pay attention to when your power animal shows up in image or actual form in your life. When it does, it's trying to get your attention about something. Some cultures are reticent about sharing their power animal identities. Others do it quite freely, so there is no hard-and-fast rule. Do what seems comfortable, but treat your power animal connection as the sacred thing it is.

◈ STONE AGE WISDOM PRACTICE #15:
Middle-World Journey— Animal Shape-Shifting Ceremony

You can use a middle-world journey in conjunction with a preparatory ceremony to explore the process of animal shape-shifting. Before beginning, you will need to decide which animal you are going to shift into and why. You should have a specific purpose in mind. This might be as simple as shape-shifting into your power animal to more deeply explore what it has to teach you. You might be facing a new challenge at work and have need of a different kind of energy. If a journey has suggested getting in touch with the power of hawk or opossum, you might use a shape-shifting process to integrate the power of these animals into your waking life. Try to find a representation of the animal into which you are going to shape-shift. Sculptures are best, but photographs and drawings will also work. Study your animal for several days prior to the shape-shift.

Costumes, masks, power objects made from a particular animal, and medicine bags are symbolic ways of accepting the animal spirit into your energy field. If you choose to use these tools, have them available. If you have multiple pieces, you can lay them out in front of you, ready to slowly be taken on as the shape-shift deepens. Define your sacred space (see chapter 7). You might want to burn sage or cedar incense, lower the lights (candlelight works best), and prepare your environment with any sensual clues that suggest the environment your power animal is used to. It is easy to find CDs of nature sounds these days. You might want the sound of the ocean in the background for a shape-shift into dolphin, whale, or seagull. Forest sounds might make bear, cougar, or raccoon right at home. Jungle sounds might invoke the spirit of jaguar or python.

Eventually, however, you will want to shift to your drumming CD. This could be as seamless as having the nature sounds on the stereo and slipping your personal sound system headphones over your ears. That way the nature sounds would still be present at the end of the experience. Whether or not you are going to shape-shift into your power animal, you can still summon its presence for protection and guidance.

As the drumming starts and you begin to relax, imagine yourself rising up out of your body. Just as you did in the middle-world journey described in the last chapter, shed your physical form and experience yourself floating in the air. Turn to look back at yourself. See your physical shell. Now look at your dreambody. You will see that it is made of a kind of liquid light. It can take on and fill any form it is poured into. If you feel a sense of panic, remember that you are connected to and part of the universal field of energy. You cannot get lost. You can return to your body at any time. You are simply shifting your luminous body from one vessel to another.

In the middle world, call the animal into which you want to shape-shift, and it will appear. To make room for your luminous body, part of the dreambody of the animal will reside in your form. This is a true exchange. Slowly pour your light body into the waiting animal, allowing time to adjust to the new sensations. Notice how your perceptions have changed. Do you have more acute senses? How do you want to move? How would you defend yourself as this animal? How would you express yourself? Is there a single primary urge that drives your existence?

Remember the intention of this journey. Were there questions you wanted to ask yourself from a new perspective? What were you tracking through this shape-shift? What did you hope to learn or experience?

You may move only in spirit form or you may find your consciousness shifting back and forth between your physical form, which is now sharing space with the animal's luminous body, and your spirit body. You may move as either one or you may move as both. You may experience the perception that while you are sharing your physical body with this animal spirit it is somewhere off in its natural habitat sharing its physical body with yours. Normal distinctions of time and space will tend to dissolve. You may have a big experience or you may have a subtle experience, but you will have an experience.

When you begin to have difficulty concentrating or when your senses begin to seem fuzzy, it is time to return to your body. Feel your luminous body pouring back into your physical body as the animal spirit returns to its physical form. This will not be a difficult process. Your animal spirit ally will be as anxious to return to its original form as you are to get back to yours.

After you are fully back in your body, ground yourself with some deep breaths, some water, and something sweet. I'm not sure why, but sugar or sweet tastes always seem to help people ground after out-of-body work.

❖ STONE AGE WISDOM PRACTICE #16:

Shape-Shifting with People

The idea of shape-shifting with other people may seem strange, but it is actually one of the most useful techniques we can learn. When we shape-shift with another person, our goal is to merge with that other person to see the world from their perspective. This might improve our ability to recognize a pattern, heal a physical condition, or break down an energetic block. It might help us better understand a conflict or the role someone is play-ing within an energetic field.

Many psychics and intuitives do this kind of shape-shifting without thinking about it. Sometimes gifted empaths do it unconsciously. Our goal is to learn to merge with someone's energy body long enough to learn from that pattern or use our own patterns to shift their patterns in a healing direction. This kind of shape-shifting is a form of energetic entrainment. To do it successfully requires a strong sense of self and a willingness to own personal power. It also requires the fundamental attitudes that have served us well in journeying: clear intention, compassion, and discipline. You need to be clear about your intention so that your reason for shape-shifting isn't motivated by selfish, egocentric concerns. You need compassion, because at a critical moment you will need to verify that your action is appropriate for the higher good. Finally, you will need discipline to avoid becoming lost and essentially useless in the shape-shifting process.

Begin by focusing your attention on the person you want to shape-shift or merge with. They may be present or you may have to close your eyes and invoke them from memory. Get a clear picture of your subject in your mind. Begin to breathe deeply, filling your body with light (see the Windhorse Breath exercise described in chapter 7). Once your body feels like it's glowing and tingling with light, allow that luminous body to step out of your physical body. Your luminous body is infinitely malleable. It can flow into any form, following the energetic map of the other person's luminous body. Let your luminous body merge with your subject. Feel your emotional, spiritual, mental, and physical patterns moving into alignment, but don't identify with them completely. You need to maintain awareness of how you are different. If you are shape-shifting from a place of compassion, the merging will flow easily. Fear, judgment, anger, or criticism will interfere with your ability to be effective. As you might guess, these emotions create separation rather than integration. The less success you have integrating, the less influence you will have.

Once you have achieved this state of merged consciousness, it is important to check in with your higher heart. Simply ask if this action is appropriate. If it is wrong to proceed, you will know it. If it is in the best interests of both parties, you will feel that, as well. If your answer is to proceed, continue to merge to the greatest degree possible. If your intention is to repattern the subject to assist in their physical, mental, emotional, or spiritual healing, now is the time to do so. If your intention is to more deeply understand your subject's behavior, patterns, desires, or perspective, now is the time to explore these areas. If your intention is to repattern your own behavior after the subject's for your personal growth and development, do it now. You can't be certain of how long you will be able to maintain this shape-shift. Once you have met the goal of your intention, imagine your luminous body returning to your own physical body.

If you experience fear or loss of focus in the process of shape-shifting with another person, you need to invoke discipline. Because fear creates separation, it's unlikely you'll be able to influence the other person's energy body, but you might inadvertently pick up negative patterns in your own energy field. For this reason it is important that you do not drift or lose focus during the process. If you feel fear or if you feel you are patterning something negative, tell yourself firmly that this is not your stuff and you will not accept it.

I use this form of shape-shifting when I am in situations where I begin to pick up double signals from someone or when I have the sense that there is something I'm not understanding about what someone is saying. I also use it when I participate in or listen to conversations in which it is clear that both parties are arguing about different things and neither party is actually hearing the other.

Fundamentally, shape-shifting is about moving energy. If I can find the place where the energy is not moving in any conflict or challenge, I am halfway to resolving it. Recognizing that it is the nature of all things to move, grow, change, die, dissolve, expand, or shift tells us that anything that restricts change is working against the true nature of those things. Shape-shifting can help us understand the true nature of things.

> *I dream that Albert Einstein is writing a formula on a blackboard with white chalk. He writes "R − pR = E−". He explains that "R" stands for reality and "pR" represents what we think reality should be. When the difference between the two is great, the energy we are losing on a daily basis around a specific issue is high. He adds that most of us spend our depleted energy continually trying to change "R" (reality) rather than reevaluating "pR" (our sense of what reality should be). We should, he further explains, always work to ensure the highest functional level of energy first, because this is where the power to influence our world comes from.*

I have increasingly come to appreciate an approach to the world around me (both the seen and the unseen) that looks to observe and describe first, without jumping to interpretation and the assignment of meaning or significance. I have come to believe that this is a fundamentally shamanic way of interacting with the world. When things annoy and irritate me, I first ask what is it that is actually happening. I vision-shift. I shape-shift. My irritation usually grows from my sense that something different should be happening. When I bring what I think should be happening into alignment with what actually is happening without attaching meaning or making assumptions, I find that I have more energy and a clearer picture of my circumstances.

Shape-shifting may have uses in situations you hadn't considered before. In situations of group dynamics, there are almost always fields in play and dreamspirits looking for voices to express them. Shape-shifting as a leader can mean the willingness to stay in motion, to not be locked into one position. Shape-shifting can mean doing the unexpected or giving voice to something that is not being expressed. Shape-shifting into animal forms can help us tap into energies and attitudes that may be foreign to us but become suddenly necessary in situations where energy is not being allowed to move. I have seen group situations where one person has been snarling with wounded-tiger ferocity. Everyone stood by stunned and cowering until the least-likely person managed to shape-shift into tiger as well and answer roar for roar until the wounded tiger finally felt heard.

Shape-shifting into human forms can help us see from a new perspective or even from multiple new perspectives. A form of shape-shifting that is common in the shamanic tradition is embracing your opponent. Often those people who seem most opposed to us in dreams and in waking life can be allies in disguise. Whether they realize it or not, they may be Spirit's messengers to help us break through a block or move energy in a way that we desperately need. This recognition of allies helps us transform.

A woman named Diane brought me a story of how over the past two years a woman had been gradually stealing her identity. The woman usually seemed rude and aloof, except when she wanted to know where Diane bought her shoes and clothes and jewelry. Invariably, the next time Diane saw this woman she was dressed in her clothes. She cut her hair like Diane's and seemed to be trying to copy her look completely. Diane expressed the feeling that this woman was throwing knives at her, and there was a lot of tension between them. I asked her to treat this like a dream and to describe where she was being stabbed. She gestured to her solar plexus (even though she said it was her heart). I trusted her body's reaction and we talked about what it would mean energetically if a dreamspirit gradually took her identity then tried to stab or cut her in the place we connect with identity and personal history. Could this woman be an ally? Could she be a worthy opponent who was saying it was time to disconnect from a story that was not serving Diane any longer? I asked about the situations in which she saw this woman in real life and learned that it was always related to picking her daughter up from school. This suggested that the identity that was not serving Diane well, the story that might need to be changed, was the one that begins "Diane the mother…."

This shift in perspective was not easy at first, but to her credit, she did not fight it. Instead she tried it on to see if it fit. Somehow she realized that she felt better about the situation with the woman and about her own issues when she could consider the woman an ally. Notice that this did not require forgiveness or acceptance of the woman's behavior on Diane's part. The energy was able to move when she shifted her perception.

Shape-shifting is also the ability to incarnate emotional states and feelings—to fully enter into an experience or to move through an experience and become the field of the experience itself. Becoming the field gives you access to something you cannot see when you are simply being moved by the field. You can see the points within any conflict at which a slight shift will profoundly alter the outcome or change the dynamic balance.

One of the most profound lessons of shape-shifting and an awareness of the truly dynamic nature of the world is the notion of change points. Understanding that energy moves and that it wants to move should free us from wasting our energy trying to hold things down and keep them as they are or as we imagine they used to be. Fundamentalist causes almost always resort to violence because they are fighting against the true nature of things. The martial artist and the shaman know that if we are perceptive and attentive to the true nature of things, we can find the change point in any situation.

The change point is that place or moment where the least amount of energy can have the biggest effect. The change points for physical disease occur in the energy template of the body long before they manifest as physical symptoms. The change points for relationships between people can be found buried in the stories neither of them is acknowledging. The change point of an emotional crisis can often be found in a homeopathic dose of the sadness, anger, or pain that has not been heard.

The sooner we track these change points, the less energy we have to apply to getting them unstuck and moving again. Finding these change points is also important because they give us something with which to work when we engage an intricately interconnected unseen world through ceremony, prayer, and sacred offerings.

Stone Age Wisdom Principles

Principle #4: The Fourth Stone

Everything is connected.

Everything exists in relationship to everything else.

Primal Alignment: Form Alliances

We learn to be respectful.

We understand sacred reciprocity.

We restore balance and harmony to all our relationships.

The Dreamer's Questions:

How am I connected to this?

How am I currently embodying this?

What is this mirroring for me?

Shamanic Practice:

Ceremony and Ritual

CHAPTER 7

Ceremony and Ritual: Mediating Between the Seen and the Unseen Worlds

*To ritualize life, we need to learn how to invoke the
spirits or things spiritual into our ceremonies.
This means being able to pray out loud, alone.
Invocation suggests that we accept the fact that
we ourselves don't know how to make things happen
they way they should. And thus we seek strength from
the spirits or Spirit by recognizing and embracing
our weakness. This way, before getting started with
any aspect of our lives—travel, a project, a meeting—
we first bring the task at hand to the attention of the
gods or God, our allies in the Otherworld.*

Malidoma Somé,
Ritual: Power, Healing, and Community

KNOWING THAT THE WORLD AROUND US is alive, conscious, and
dynamic means nothing if we do not recognize that we are intimately

and inextricably connected to everything else. It is the sense of being connected that makes the idea that the universe is alive and conscious matter at all. This is not just fanciful or wishful "New Age" thinking. It reflects the cutting edge of scientific thought. Chaos theory suggests that something as insignificant as a butterfly flapping its wings in Lhasa can affect the weather patterns in Miami. Lynne McTaggart has written about the discoveries of quantum physicists in *The Field: The Quest for the Secret Force of the Universe,* "If the Zero Point Field—an ocean of microscopic vibrations in the space between things—were included in our conception of the most fundamental nature of matter, they realized, the very underpinning of our universe was a heaving sea of energy—one vast quantum field. If this were true, everything would be connected to everything else like some invisible web."

Ritual and ceremony make the web visible. To borrow Dagara medicine carrier Malidoma Somé's definition, ceremony is to the seen world what ritual is to the unseen world. Ceremony is form; ritual is intention. Ceremony is matter; ritual is spirit. Ceremony without ritual is lifeless; ritual without ceremony is unrealized potential. Ceremony is a series of actions and gestures that become sacred—that become ritual—with the invocation and presence of the spirits or unseen forces. Ritual is about the forging of alliances. Through ritual we establish and strengthen our relationship to the members of our community, to the natural world around us, and to the unseen world of spirit and energy. Of all the goals of urban contemporary shamanism, none is more important than the return of the sacred to everyday life.

It seems appropriate in this chapter to address two of the strongest indictments against shamanism's adoption by Western urban cultures. The first is that shamans are only shamans in relationship to a community. They are not mystics or hermits. They may retreat from community for vision quests or to commune with the spirits, but their work is with community. It is the community, in fact, that confers the title of shaman on an individual. Some argue that in a culture that does not honor shamanism or shamanic ways of seeing the world and that has lost the real meaning of community, there is no place for shamanism or shamanic practitioners.

I disagree with this argument. Shamans, in their roles as ritual leaders, did more than just serve communities. Their mediation between the seen and the unseen worlds, their ability to give form to essentially formless spiritual processes, wove their communities together. It seems to me that we can lament the loss of community in our culture or we can learn from the shamans of indigenous cultures how to weave new communities. Arnold Mindell has written in *The Shaman's Body* that, "...without a shaman facilitator, individual and group processes may not unravel constructively. Nowhere are there enough shamans with second attention to pick up double signals or practice controlled abandon. There are always too few people around who are sufficiently humble to help the rest of the people move in and out of spirits in a field."

Rather than trying to preserve shamanism as something foreign, exotic, and altogether other, we need to learn how the shaman's rituals can serve the creation of new communities. These communities may look different than the tribes and hunter-gatherer bands of our Stone Age ancestors, but I believe it is in our blood to seek inclusive communities in which wise elders and shamanic caretakers ensure that all voices are heard.

The second argument against the usefulness of shamanism is that the indigenous shaman is successful because he or she is so connected to the wild natural world. The shaman's role and power derive from his or her role as an intermediary between the human community and the natural landscape. Most urban Westerners are not intimately aware of the rhythms and cycles of the natural world, so some critics suggest that this urban form of shamanism can be only a pale imitation.

Perhaps I could allow a traditional shaman to answer this criticism. My friend Maria Volchenko shared with me what her Tuvan shamanic teacher told her. Maria lives in Moscow and travels to the remote region of Tuva to study and learn from the master shamans who survived the repression of the Soviet government. "I think your job as a shaman is much more difficult than mine," her teacher once commented to her. "When I need to call the spirits, all I have to do is look out my window. The spirits of the trees, the mountains, the fields, the lakes, and the rivers are right here. You shamans who live in the city must have a harder time of calling in spirit. You've paved everything over and the spirits get lost trying to find their way to you. The rituals you perform, the altars you build, the sacred ground you consecrate, and the offerings you make are the only way spirit can find you."

I appreciate this assessment, because it does not claim that shamanic values are useless, worthless, or ineffective in the city, just that the form the practice takes will look different and that there will be challenges to overcome. It may also be that contemporary shamanic practitioners can help their communities return to a sense of respect and reciprocal relationship to the Earth.

I also appreciate the arguments against urban contemporary shamanism and the people that make them. These people are usually trying to protect something they value highly and are wary of our culture's ability to co-opt and trivialize. Their criticisms have helped me better shape my ideas and have encouraged me to be vigilant and responsible. In the end, however, I have seen too many instances of profound healing and realignment coming from urban contemporary shamanic practices to dismiss the phenomenon.

The lesson of the Fourth Stone is that everything is related. From this lesson we learn to be respectful, to understand sacred reciprocity, and to realize that through ritual we can restore balance and harmony to all our relationships. To the urban shaman, relationship is everything.

Ritual works because of relationship. Ritual is a way of influencing the energy fields toward positive outcomes. Repeating a positive pattern enough times can overwrite the script on any given energetic field. We can heal and transform ourselves through ritual, and, what is even more extraordinary, we may actually heal others in the process. Leslie Kenton has written in *Journey to Freedom* that "Ritual is a way of connecting us with sacred energy and then shaping and directing it to a particular end. Like morphic fields which, although we can not see them, affect the material world, the shapeshifting energy that is carried by our intentions as we go through sacred rituals connects up clear lines of power between quantum realms and ordinary reality."

In Western cultures we have intellectually cut ourselves free from the web of the world. We don't see ourselves as connected to family, community, or the land. We have refuted the idea that we are physically or spiritually connected, and so we are also free of any responsibility. We live by intellect, separate and alone, relating to other separate and lone individuals in a lifeless world. This is not a pretty picture.

Fortunately, it is not the only way. In Peru there is an expression known as *ayni*. This literally means, "today for me, tomorrow for you." Ayni is what you owe your community, your fellow human beings, and the seen and unseen world around you. Ayni is about being in reciprocal relationships. Ayni is the practice of sacred reciprocity. One of the classic roles of the shaman is to mediate between the seen and the unseen worlds. This is most often done through ritual. Ritual is a way of manifesting the unseen world. Through ceremony we bring tangible symbols of the essential elements—often earth, air, fire, and water—together with other symbols for the unseen world. By invoking, beseeching, negotiating with, feeding, and appeasing these elements, we influence the unseen world and the very patterns that are shaping our lives in the seen world. The shaman is a master at balancing the relationship between the seen and the unseen worlds.

There are many kinds of rituals and many ritual traditions. One chapter cannot adequately cover the subject of ritual. We can, however, explore the ways in which ritual serves our awareness of an interconnected world. In addition, we can look at some specific examples of rituals with very practical purposes. In fact, the Dagara of Africa would not understand the idea of a ritual that did not have a very practical purpose or goal in mind. Again, Somé writes, "Consequently, each time we enter a ritual space we do so because something in the physical world has warned us of possible deterioration at hand. This presupposes that one does not enter into a ritual without a purpose, a goal. As I said earlier, ritual is called for because our soul communicates things to us that the body translates as need, or want, or absence. So we enter into ritual to respond to the call of the soul...Purpose is the driving force that contributes to the effectiveness of ritual."

The shaman enters a rustic room in a house near the village of Huautla de Jimenez in the mountains of Oaxaca, Mexico. This is the village of the legendary Mazatec curandera, Maria Sabina, who introduced the sacred mushroom ceremony to R. Gordon Wasson and Allan Richardson in 1955. The diminutive shaman has come to perform a healing ceremony, or velada.

He clears off a tiny table to use as an altar and lays out his tools. Candles, feathers, herbs, eggs and other items are neatly arranged. He unwraps a packet of freshly gathered mushrooms (Psilocybe caerulescens var. mazatecorum) *and begins to count them out into pairs of male and female mushrooms on banana leaf plates.*

He diagnoses each of the participants in the ceremony, determining what needs to be healed or balanced. He purifies himself and the participants with aromatic herbs and billowing copal incense. He prays and invokes the presence of the mushroom spirits and the gods that will watch over the participants.

The mushrooms are consumed and the lights turned out. Within minutes the participants come into the presence of the divine mushroom spirit. For hours, the shaman sings, prays, and shepherds the participants through the process. His only breaks are when he steps outside to cough or wretch up the toxic spirits and negative energies he has drawn from the participants with the help of the mushrooms. Though the preparations had not appeared elaborate, they were enough to create a safe vessel for the release of the things each participant was holding. An incredible sense of camaraderie is created among the participants. Energies

are aligned and blocks are cleared. As the ritual draws to a
close after six or seven hours, the shaman expresses gratitude
to the spirits and releases them. The ritual is closed and the
shaman ensures that the energetic changes everyone has
experienced have been integrated.

Different spiritual traditions have forms their rituals follow, and the shamanic tradition is no exception. The idea of traveling or journeying pervades the shamanic ritual model. There is a sense in which the participants agree to make a healing journey together, whether as a community or in support of an individual. The shaman functions as something of an alternate-reality tour guide and leader. He knows the territory and has an obligation to keep everyone safe and ensure that no one gets left behind. There are seven steps to the shamanic ritual.

1. Intention: the shaman and the participants agree
   on the purpose of the ritual.
2. Consecration: the shaman invokes sacred space.
3. Purification: the shaman cleanses and purifies herself
   and the participants.
4. Invocation: the shaman calls the spirits.
5. Action: the proper ceremonial action is given form.
6. Appreciation: the shaman thanks the spirits and
   releases them.
7. Integration: the shaman helps the participants
   return to daily life.

This sequence is essential to the process of creating a ritual for others, but the steps themselves can also serve a personal goal of returning the sacred quality to everyday life. As we look at the steps, we will consider some Stone Age Wisdom Practices that can function as part of a greater ritual or as ritual elements for day-to-day living.

Step 1: Intention

As with all the practices we have examined—dreaming, vision-shifting, journeying, and shape-shifting—intention is critical. We must have a purpose and a reason for the ritual we perform. There are many reasons to have rituals. There are natural cycles of the Earth in relationship to the sun, the moon, and the planets that need to be honored. We can honor the summer and winter solstices, the vernal and autumnal equinoxes, the full and new moons, and planetary alignments. Rituals like this help us reconnect to the natural rhythms of the seasons. We can take advantage of holidays that allow us to set aside time to focus on different processes of life. Samhain or Halloween can be a time for mourning the things that have died for us in the past year, just as Easter or May Day can celebrate birth and new beginnings.

Sometimes when you are making a transition to a more sacred way of living, it can seem more manageable to focus on specific days around which to create ritual observances. Start out with the solstices and the equinoxes. When that feels comfortable, add in other special days. In my family, we've made a special holiday event out of the winter solstice. We exchange simple gifts of personal or spiritual significance. It has helped weave new family members in and it honors the special time. The children love it. It has become a time to focus on something other than the whirlwind of presents that marks Christmas. Eventually you may find yourself organizing full moon and other ceremonies.

There are also the rituals of transition. Births, naming ceremonies, coming of age, graduation, marriage, ordination, menopause, death, and times of great change all cry out to be honored through ritual. As a high school teacher for a number of years, I saw firsthand how damaging it is to children that we have no formal coming of age ritual. This important time is not honored, and the only way we mark the passage into adulthood is by eliminating the list of things children are not allowed to do: smoke, drink alcohol, drive, own firearms, and have sex. Is it any wonder that younger and younger children grasp at these culturally approved signs of adulthood? And what about the man who spends all his life becoming a wise elder in the community of work? Once he begins to develop real wisdom, he is retired and shifted to a field in which his "work wisdom" is useless and he is not needed anymore. Is it surprising that men often die soon after retiring?

The kinds of rituals shamans practice most often are rituals of gratitude and rituals of rebalancing. The shaman builds alliances through gratitude, sacred offerings, and ritual feedings of the Earth and the spirits. The more alliances a shaman has, the more power is available to be directed toward healing or resolving issues for the community. Rebalancing rituals help individuals heal by increasing their levels of personal power and withdrawing any harmful foreign intruders.

The intention for a ritual may be formalized according to a calendar (for example, the Day of the Dead in Mexico calls for certain prescribed events), or it may require research. A shaman faced with a client who is ill may need to study the client's energy field by vision-shifting, dreaming about the illness, journeying to seek spirit guidance, or shape-shifting to see the problem from the inside out. The symptoms themselves are of interest, but the same symptoms in two different individuals may lead to different diagnoses.

In creating a ritual, you may use any of these techniques. You may also want to talk to the participants and come to a group consensus about the purpose and intention of the ritual. It is important that the participants understand the intention of the ritual as well as the reasons for certain actions. After all, what you really want is to be able to harness the collective will for the benefit of the individual or the community. Once the intention is set, you can prepare yourself energetically for the next step with the following two practices.

◈ STONE AGE WISDOM PRACTICE #17:
Windhorse Breathwork

Windhorse is the way Mongolian shamanism expresses the idea of personal power, medicine, or psychic energy. Developing Windhorse means that the individual has the personal reserves of strength and energy to accomplish spiritual, ritual, or healing work. One of the ways shamans around the world increase their energy levels is through focused work with the breath. Breath is considered to be one of the principle ways of directing Spirit or energy. Shamans suck out harmful entities and bestow blessings with breath. Breath carries prayer, whether on the back of sacred smoke, misted liquids, whistling, chanting, speaking or singing. Breath animates stones and sacred objects and transfers energy. Breath circulates energy in the body and pumps it in and out through points of connection with the heavens and the Earth. The purpose of Windhorse Breathwork is threefold:

1. To cleanse and clear dense energy.
2. To fortify the energy system through the deliberate intake and distribution of lifeforce energy (chi or prana).

3. To make one a better carrier of spirit medicine and
   develop Windhorse.

The breathwork described below uses pauses for retention and
gradually lengthens the inhalation/retention/exhalation time.
Lengthening the inhalation time and capacity increases the intake
of energy through your breath. Extending the retention time
(holding) allows for energy to be separated from air and stored in
the appropriate chakras. Lengthening the exhalation time allows
one to make more room in the energy body by releasing toxins and
impurities, as well as directing energy to storage loci for later use.

1. Begin with Wave Breath: Inhale for 7 seconds. Retain for 1 second.
Let your exhalation follow naturally like a wave cresting. Exhale
for 7 seconds. Pause for 1 second. Repeat. This should have you
breathing at about 4 breaths per minute. Simply visualize energy
(prana or chi) as a force being drawn into your body with each
inhalation. On the exhalation, feel this energy spreading through
your body. Repeat for 4 minutes.

2. Continue the Wave Breath, but pause for 7 seconds during
each retention, turning this into Earth Energy Breath. This pattern
connects you with the Earth. It is controlled, without being too
strenuous. It is the best breath for building physical energy, as it
helps you remain in your body, focused and present. Visualize Earth
energy being drawn up from the Earth through the soles of your
feet, your perineum, and the palms of your hands on each inhalation.
As you inhale, visualize blue-green light coming up from the center
of the Earth. Feel this energy as a warm, vibrant, nurturing force. Fill
your *qosqo* (kush-ko) or sacral chakra (located 3 inches below your
navel) with this energy. As you retain your breath, feel it circulate
within you. As you exhale, feel it return to the Earth, carrying away

heavy, dense energy and impurities. See it feeding the Earth. Feel your own lightness. This should take about 2 minutes.

3. Next, lengthen your inhale/retain/exhale sequence to intervals of 10/10/10, 15/15/15, or 20/20/20 seconds. Visualize the energy bubble surrounding you. It will be about 6 feet in diameter and more egg-shaped than circular. If you can see a clear picture of it or feel it strongly, just note what condition it is in. Now as you inhale, visualize a beam of radiant light entering through the crown of your head and dropping down to your heart. At the same time, continue to visualize the Earth energy moving up through your legs, feet, and perineum, but now bring it up into your heart to merge with the beam of light coming down through your crown. On your retention, feel this strengthening, protective, empowering energy concentrate as a dazzling, glowing ball of light. On your exhalation, send this energy out into your energy bubble. Feel it infuse and energize you. Continue this for 4 minutes.

4. As you reach the point of one long, slow breath per minute, close your eyes and look up with your physical eyes to the third eye point between your eyebrows. Strain your eyes slightly by looking as far up and back as you can. Hold this position for as long as it is comfortable, then hold it a little longer. With each inhalation, visualize energy coming up from the Earth and down from the heavens, passing through your body to meet at your third eye. Hold to build the energy. As you exhale, spin the energy in a vortex extending out from your third eye. You should now be close to the point of transcendent detachment, able to witness your actions without identifying with them. Be open to what spiritual guidance comes. Continue this for 2 minutes.

5. Gradually return your breathing to intervals of 10/10/10 seconds, and then allow it to find its own natural rhythm.

☸ STONE AGE WISDOM PRACTICE #18:

Centering

Most shamanic practitioners honor, in some way, the four cardinal directions of north, south, east, and west. They also usually honor the directions up and down, and sometimes the direction of inside is also honored. Various medicine wheel or sacred circle cosmologies assign different qualities to the directions. When we honor or call in the directions, we often use these qualities to refer to the directions because it seems more practical or less abstract. If I'm asking for fire energy from the east, that seems like more of a reason for invoking the directions.

While I use a Peruvian set of associations of energies that coincide with the elements, I think that the directions themselves have something more substantial to offer us. In his book *Re-Visioning the Earth: A Guide to Opening the Healing Channels Between Mind and Nature,* Paul Devereux writes that the importance of the four or six directions is what happens at the convergence point. That point is the center—the umbilicus of the universe. In essence, we honor the directions, marking them in relationship to ourselves, to find our center point. By tracking the directions and finding ourselves at the intersection, we place ourselves back at the center of the universe. In Devereux's words:

> But who or what stands at the crossroads of the Four Directions? Cognitive science says that there is no such actual entity as a self or an ego; it is simply a useful image conjured by the machinations of the brain-mind. So there is only a mirage, a ghost, at the crossroads. Ancient tribal wisdom says much the same thing, but in another, richer way, and with infinitely greater implications than

modern science can find its way to seeing. This wisdom and knowledge take us one final stage deeper—to the center of the Center, to the core mystery around which it all revolves. To zero point.

This zero point is the axis of north, south, east, west, above, and below. At the zero point, the only way to go is within. We access this axial element at the center by way of ecstatic states of consciousness. The shamanic journey, if it is to be experienced rather than forced, must begin at this center point. So, when we align ourselves to the directions, it is not simply to tap the energies or aspects we have attached to those directions, but more importantly, to align ourselves—returning to center to find our point of embarkation for the unseen world.

Again, to quote Devereux:

This fundamental experience of transformed human consciousness is at the heart of the World Center myth. Encircling that is the experience of perception and cognition related to the physical world, the middle world of shamanic tradition. In a wider circle around that are the projections of physical orientation, origin myths, and cosmologies. But we must not lose sight of the fact that, though the concept of the omphalos *(world navel) and* axis mundi *(world tree or pole) was an exoteric (symbolic and ceremonial) construct for most societies, for the shaman it was a metaphor for a concrete experience. Only shamans and others who experience the prima ecstatic state are conscious at the center of the world.*

Centering Ritual

In practice, it might be wise to take some time to simply honor the directions for the way they allow us to find that axial intersection, to find ourselves at the center of the world.

1. Stand with your feet shoulder-width apart and parallel. Standing barefoot on the Earth is best if you can arrange it; at the very least, avoid hard-soled shoes and elevated heels. Let your arms hang loosely at your sides.

2. Sway gently from your left foot to your right, side to side, trying to feel what it feels like to have all your weight on one foot and then the other. Come to a resting point when you have an absolutely equal amount of weight on each leg. We often unconsciously stand with more weight on one leg. This side-to-side balancing helps us align.

3. Now rock gently back and forth, shifting your weight from the balls of your feet to your heels. Do not lift your heels or the balls of your feet off the floor. This is a subtle process. Come to rest with your weight distributed equally between the fronts and the backs of your feet.

4. Now, with your weight evenly distributed back and forward, left and right, you will become aware of matching energy centers in the arches of your feet opening up channels to draw energy up from the Earth (left foot and leg) and to send energy back into the Earth (right foot and leg).

5. Feel this energy concentrate in your qosqo or spiritual stomach, a point inside you equidistant from your belly and your back, about 3 inches below your naval.

6. Visualize a line passing through this point, extending out in front of you and back behind you into infinity.

7. Visualize a line bisecting the first line and extending out to either side of you into infinity. The intersection of these two lines creates a point that locates you absolutely in two-dimensional space.

8. Visualize a third line extending up from that point, through the crown of your head, and down into the Earth. You are now bisected by three lines and six directions: before and behind, to the left and the right, above and below. This locates you absolutely in three-dimensional space-time.

9. Finally, allow your consciousness bubble to descend to that center inside you and take the only direction left: within. You are now at the sacred center of the universe, present and ready to conduct ritual.

Step 2: Consecration

Both Windhorse Breathwork and Centering are powerful practices in their own rights. They are useful as preparations for ritual or to stay energized, balanced, and aware of the sacred from day to day. Consecration is the act of making a place sacred or awakening the sacred in a place. It, too, can be applied in many ways.

Consecration is essential to ritual because ritual without a sacred container is neither safe nor effective. Ritual without a consecrated container would be like asking for water in the desert: Without a container to catch and hold it in, the water would wash over you and disappear into the sand without ever quenching your thirst.

When we consecrate, we are dedicating a place and a period of time to sacred or meaningful work. Some consecration is temporary. I sometimes arrive early for business conferences so that I have time to consecrate the meeting space. It is not that there is anything particularly sacred about what will go on at the meeting, but in consecrating the space I am admitting that things will be better done if Spirit is present. Malidoma Somé writes in *Ritual: Power, Healing, and Community,* "A sacred life is a ritualized life, that is, one that draws constantly from the realm of the spiritual to handle even the smallest situation."

I consecrate the spaces I will be doing medicine work in, even if they are temporary. I have places in my home and office that are consecrated more permanently in recognition that I do sacred work there on a regular basis. Then there are the already sacred and consecrated places that I visit. Sometimes I reconsecrate them, not so much because they need my attention but because the cumulative effect of repeated consecration makes ground more sacred and more powerful.

◈ STONE AGE WISDOM PRACTICE #19:

Consecrating Sacred Ground

Consecrating ground can be done very simply or very elaborately, but the power really comes from your intention to consecrate, to mark out a special place in time and space where the sacred will be honored.

To consecrate the ground for an important conversation, sit quietly for a moment with the person with whom you'll be speaking. Ask for the ability to both listen and speak from your heart without blame, judgment, or attachment. Then light a candle between you. Something as simple and as alive as a dancing candle flame can focus the energy of the conversation and invite the presence of Spirit.

To consecrate an area of your home for an altar or to consecrate the ground at the center of a scared circle for a ritual, gather the following ingredients:

- blue or yellow cornmeal
- tobacco
- three dried or fresh leaves from a tree or shrub native to the place you are consecrating
- clear spirits or flower water

1. Take some cornmeal in your right hand. Hold it to your belly, your heart, and your third eye as you commit to contributing your physical, emotional, and mental energy to the ritual. Breathe gently into the cornmeal to add your spiritual energy.

2. Beginning in the south or the east (whichever feels most comfortable to you), make a small circle with the cornmeal. As you do this, acknowledge the sacred container you are creating as well as the circular nature of time.

3. Take some tobacco in your right hand and touch it to your belly, your heart, and your third eye, invoking physical, emotional, and mental energy. Breathe into it gently to add your spiritual energy. Beginning at the north edge of the circle, make the north-south arm of a cross as you acknowledge the desire to bring Spirit (from the north) into physical form (in the south). The north-south arm is the spirit arm of the cross. It recognizes your incarnation of Spirit in a physical body.

4. Repeat step 3, but this time make an east-west arm of the cross while acknowledging the linear aspect of time, from birth to death, from beginning to end. The east-west arm of the cross is the soul arm and acknowledges the restriction of time and the importance of using it well.

5. Take the three leaves and arrange them so the bases of the leaves overlap but the tips of the leaves fan out. Breathe across them lightly to acknowledge the three worlds and the three

energies: upper, middle, and lower; mental, emotional, and physical. Place them in the center of the cross to invoke a doorway between the three worlds.

6. Give the center of the cross a few drops of clear spirits or flower water to acknowledge the Earth Mother.

You may now lay an altar cloth over this consecrated ground and continue with the ritual.

⬧ STONE AGE WISDOM PRACTICE #20:

The Ritual Altar

Once you have consecrated your ground, you can lay out your ritual altar. I'm going to suggest that you begin by creating a kind of portable altar called a Mesa. Many shamanic traditions have variations of portable or more permanent altars. This altar is based on the Peruvian shamanic tradition. It is an adaptation of the Mesa as taught by Don Oscar Miro-Quesada. More information about it can be found in Matthew Magee's book *Peruvian Shamanism: The Pachakúti Mesa.* This is a tradition I know and trust, and it has seemed to work well for my students. This altar can be transported easily (unless you feel the need to have really heavy or bulky objects on your Mesa) and is simple to learn. To create it you will need the following items:

A piece of cloth about 24 inches square. Select something that pleases you visually and sensually. Shamans in Peru carry their sacred items in cloth bundles of beautiful woven fabrics. These bundles have to be tough because they must carry stones and heavy objects and because they are constantly being carried from place to place. You can also choose a piece of cloth that has sentimental meaning for you. If you don't like what you have now, set the intention to find something new and see what happens.

The Mesa cloth, or *manta*, is laid over the consecrated ground (the cornmeal circle and tobacco cross), with the straight edges aligned to the cardinal directions.

A stone or crystal. This piece will hold the element of Earth and the energy of the body, and of physical and material things. It will sit in the south of your Mesa.

A seashell or a bowl of water. This will hold the element of water and the energy of the heart, and of emotional and relationship issues. It will sit in the west of your Mesa.

A feather. This will hold the element of air, wind, or breath, and the energy of Spirit and divine guidance. It will sit in the north of your Mesa.

A white candle. This will hold the element of fire and mental energy, vision, and clarity. It will sit in the east of your Mesa.

A centerpiece consisting of three items. The base will be a flat shell or bowl representing the lower world and what we learn from the spirits and teachers of the lower world and from our own past. The next level will be a flat tile or slab of stone that represents the middle world and what we learn from our living teachers and mentors. The third level will be a cross representing the upper world and what we learn from the higher powers and the future. (In Peru, you often see a crucifix in this position because shamans, who once used the equidistant cross, adopted the crucifix to appease the colonial Catholic priests.) The centerpiece symbolizes the gateway between worlds and the balancing of the four energies and elements.

As you place each object, open your left palm to the heavens and direct your right palm to the object. Feel the energy of the element you are invoking move in through your left palm, travel across your heart and down your right arm to be directed out your right palm.

You may wish to chant, sing, or speak the names of the elements you are invoking in English or in Quechua (the ancient language of the Andes): Earth (*Allpa*), water (*unu*), air or wind (*wayra*), fire (*nina*), and Rainbow Spirit Guardian of the Center (*K'uychi*).

As you work your way around, you should feel the energy in your Mesa begin to bubble and tingle. You may add items of personal spiritual significance to your Mesa, but avoid adding things just for show. Only add things that have meaning and that hold energies you wish to summon. There is a lot of depth in this altar despite its simplicity. The most important thing to remember is that it is designed to be a kind of map that gives form to the sacred. It is your personal intersection between worlds. It is called the Pachakúti Mesa. Pachakúti means "world reversal" or "time of great change." The Mesa is your surfboard for times of dramatic change. It will help you stay flexible and move with the energy of change, rather than trying to fight it.

With the Mesa, you are always seeking balance on the south-north axis between the element of Earth (divine feminine energy in stillness) or matter and air (divine masculine energy in stillness) or spirit. Too much attention to the body and the material world means living without spirit. Too much attention to spiritual matters means ignoring the physical experience of being born into a body with a finite amount of time.

You also strive for balance on the east-west axis between water (the divine feminine energy in motion) or heart and fire (the divine masculine energy in motion) or mind. If you live too much in your heart, you are subject to the constant flooding of emotion. If you live too much in your head, you organize and repress, thinking when you need to be feeling.

In addition to using your Mesa as a focal point for ritual, it is a good practice to sit with it for a little while each day. Light your candle in the east and perhaps light some incense. Invoke the energies of the elements and ask them for guidance and support in the things you have to do during the day. Mark significant changes in your life or new revelations by adding objects to your Mesa. Place symbols of your dreams on your Mesa. Add an image or a likeness of your power animal. Place photographs of loved ones, especially those to whom you wish to direct healing energy, on your Mesa in the appropriate areas: south for physical healing, west for emotional healing, north for spiritual healing, and east for mental healing or increased clarity or vision. Create a symbol or designate a stone to represent yourself. Place the stone on the Mesa according to the kind of energy you need in order to return to a place of balance. Use your Mesa to give form to your prayers.

Step 3: Purification

Before beginning any ritual, a symbolic cleansing needs to occur. Churches often have bowls of water near their entrances for anointing and spiritual cleansing. In Eastern temples, shoes are left outside and feet are washed before entering the ritual space.

This cleansing serves at least two purposes. In a very real sense, we pick up dense, dark, heavy energy during our ordinary interactions of any given day. This energy is not necessarily evil or malevolent, but it is too heavy for us to process effectively, so it begins to clog our energy body and weigh us down. The cleansing process clears away the residue of our recent experiences, making us fresh and clear for the ritual. Cleansing does not heal, but it ensures that a healing can occur more effectively because the subject is clear and the healer or the spirits can more easily access the energetic cause of the problem. When you have been successfully cleansed, you feel a little lighter and clearer than you just did. You experience a quick attitude adjustment.

This leads to the second reason for the cleansing. The cleansing, whether done with smoke or water, or by sweeping the aura or using some tool to pull heavy energy out, helps the participant shift his or her frame of reference from the mundane to the sacred. The little cleansing ritual marks out a threshold that must be crossed before entering into the ritual space. Standing in a line quietly as you watch the healer pass fragrant smoke in and around the energy body of one person after another moves you into a receptive state and defines the necessary before and after borders.

Cleansing can be a very simple process or it can be more elaborate. One of the simplest methods of cleansing is called smudging. Find some loose dried sage, a fireproof bowl lined with sand, and a feather. Sprinkle a small amount of the sage into the bowl and light the sage. You can use sage wands found in Native American and New Age stores if you're doing a lot of cleansing, but I find that a few leaves provide enough smoke for a quick cleansing without filling a room with smoke. Extinguish the flames and fan the sage with the feather. Use the feather to direct the smoke over your head, down your torso, around your back, and under your arms and legs. Don't forget to pass the soles of your feet through the smoke, too. Offer any remaining smoke to the spirits with gratitude.

You can use the smoke from sage, cedar, pine, or copal resin for cleansing. Sweetgrass and lavender will also work, but these are more often used to attract positive energies and spirits.

There are other ways of cleansing and clearing yourself or participants in a ritual. You can use rattles or bells shaken around a person. You can sweep the energy field with a feather or with a bundle of aromatic herbs or flowers (fresh rosemary or carnations or roses). Shamans in South and Central America take a small amount of alcohol or flower water into their mouths and spray it as a fine mist into the client's energy field. Find a way that feels comfortable to you and use it to cleanse yourself after a taxing day or an emotionally tense or argumentative exchange. Cleanse and clear children after fights, arguments, or difficult days at school. Cleansing or clearing yourself once a day is just good energetic hygiene. It is also a great way of bringing the sacred into everyday experience.

Step 4: Invocation

Invocation means calling the spirits and the energies to be present. Malidoma Somé writes, "Invocation is a call placed by a person to a spirit. To invoke a spirit is to call upon the invisible. The language of invocation must not be confused with order and command. It must be closer to a plea, a humble request. This is because ritual is a spirit-based activity performed by humans. For anything to happen, the ritual must be dominated by humility."

If you have set up an altar or your Mesa, you may have already invoked the spirits and the elemental energies. If not, let the objects on your altar guide you. Give voice to a heartfelt invitation to each of the elements, energies, guardian spirits, mentors, power animals, or ancestor spirits that you would like to have present. You invocation does not have to be fancy or follow any kind of arcane pattern of grammar. What matters is your intention and your attitude of respect. Unlike practitioners of some other magical spiritual traditions, shamans never command spirits or energies to be present. Would you want people at your party who were only there because someone made them come?

Step 5: Action

Action is that part of the ritual where spirit is given form. Sometimes the shaman or healer has already journeyed to diagnose the illness and to decide on the proper ceremony. On the other hand, both the diagnostic and the restorative aspects of the process may occur in the same ritual. Even if the shaman has already diagnosed the illness, he or she may still enter a trance and journey to effect a cure in the unseen realms before bridging that action into the waking world.

As part of the ritual, some process may be symbolically enacted. Two things help make the ritual more successful and effective at this point. The first is if the participants have some idea of what is going on and why things are being done. The second is if there is a way for them to actively participate and support the ritual. Without these two aspects, rituals become more like performances from which we can hold ourselves distant. In tribal settings, the rituals have all been done before and children grow up with them, so there is little need to explain. Contemporary urban shamans, though, might need to spend a few minutes explaining what is about to happen and why.

Participants in a ritual can be given active roles, such as symbolically creating a container by holding the cardinal directions. You can ask people to sing, chant, intone, or pray. You can ask people to play parts so that energies can be expressed. You can ask people to hold materials that will be needed, serve ritual food, or lead people from a threshold to a place in the circle.

It is difficult to prescribe the correct action for a ritual. If you come from a tradition with very specific rituals for certain conditions, you may choose to follow or adapt one of those. If not, you may learn about ritual actions by reading or by attending rituals.

You can learn a lot about ritual by simply attending a wedding or baptism. Look at the ritual in an energetic way. What energetic need does each of the components address? Once you have an idea of the kind of ritual that might be effective, feel free to adapt it based on intuition or divine guidance. We sometimes feel that rituals are set and must remain the same, but among people who live by ritual, there is an understanding that rituals constantly evolve based on spiritual feedback in the form of the dreams and visions of a community's members.

◈ STONE AGE WISDOM PRACTICE #21:

Ritual of Release—Cutting Ties

We need to have loving and healthy links to people. We are part of an energetic network or web, and through these positive links we exchange energy, feeding and being fed in a reciprocal relationship. Sometimes, however, our connections to others are based on less healthy dynamics, such as duty, guilt, lust, or envy. Sometimes our connections are even more toxic for us, especially when they are based on fear, anger, or the need to dominate and exert power. These relationships do not feed us, they simply drain us. A ritual to release a connection and cut a tie can also be a ritual to call part of your power and energy back.

It is a good idea to cut cords on a daily basis. This does not mean that you are cutting your connections to people you love. New connections can form easily enough. This process simply reinforces that every day, everyone you love gets a fresh start. The simple or self-administered version of this ritual is to stand with feet apart and knees slightly bent. Sensitize your hands by rubbing them together briskly. Imagine energetic power cords connecting to your body at the solar plexus area. Use large, sweeping motions of your right and left hands to gather up all of these cords in your left hand. You should feel the cords tingle as they are compressed in your hand. Briskly and forcefully chop down with the edge of your right hand, cutting through the cords close to your body. You may repeat the action several times until it feels as if the cords have been cut. Throw the cords to the side and down to the Earth to dispose of them. Direct both of your palms toward the pile of cut cords and visualize a few seconds of violet light at them to neutralize their power.

While it is possible to do private rituals where the steps are simply visualized, the most powerful rituals benefit from the energy of actually physically enacting the disconnection and having that process witnessed by others, as in the ritual below.

1. Gather a group of friends to serve as witnesses. Follow the steps of intention, consecration, purification, and invocation. Add a 6 or 8-foot coil of silver or blue string to your altar, as well as a shiny pair of scissors.

2. Have the person wishing to disconnect stand on one side of the altar or Mesa. Ask someone to stand in for the person being disconnected from. Have that person stand opposite the first person on the other side of the altar.

3. Make a protective circle of sea salt or cornmeal around each person. Tie one end of the string around the middle finger of each person's left hand. Have each person hold his left hand over his solar plexus, and have them walk backwards until the string is stretched taut.

4. Allow the person who wishes to disconnect to speak to the person from whom they wish to disconnect. The other person should remain silent and listen. This may be the only time the person

wishing to disconnect has had a chance to be heard. After he has spoken, ask him to clearly state the wish to disconnect and the reason why.

5. Hand the scissors to the person wishing to disconnect and ask that before cutting the cord he take a moment to send love and light through that connecting cord to the best of his ability. Then have him cut the cord, saying, "I release us from this pattern. We each have our energy back and we both are safe."

6. Both participants should then ball up their end of the twine to be buried or burned separately. The stand-in for the person being disconnected from may return to the circle. Ask the person remaining in the circle to notice how he or she feels. Take a few moments to process what has happened. Allow the person to give voice to his feelings and experiences. Finally, welcome the newly empowered member back into the circle.

Remember that a ritual of disconnection like this does not mean that the relationship has to end. It simply means that both parties are energetically free to choose whether they wish to have a relationship and what kind of relationship they wish it to be.

We have barely scratched the surface of what ritual is and can be. Remember that ritual is intended to help you build alliances. The more you invoke particular manifestations of the unseen world, the stronger your connection will be. You may find you have an affinity to a certain element, such as water. Honor that by invoking water energy in both the seen and the unseen worlds. Make a bath or a swim in the ocean a sacred moment. Install one of those tabletop fountains so you can hear the sound of bubbling water. Drink spring water and splash a little onto the ground as an offering to the Earth Mother.

Ritual helps you build your alliances with power animals and plant and animal spirit allies. Ritual gives these relationships form. Make a ritual out of gift-giving by consecrating the ground (remember that consecrating the ground can be as simple as lighting a candle), invoking the spirits through telling the story of the gift, and making the action be the exchange. These little everyday rituals make life sacred and shift the energy of your relationships in a profound way.

Keep in mind that the rituals you enact and the ways you caretake for the sacred and unseen world can help you build strong, healthy alliances with the people around you. It is okay to want the world around you to reflect the beauty you are discovering as you open up to the unseen. What's more, that's the way the world wants to be. We have learned to see the world the way our Stone Age ancestors saw it: as a living, conscious, dynamic, and interconnected place. Our final challenge is to understand the most radical concept of all: This living field of energy responds to even the simplest of prayers.

Stone Age Wisdom Principles

Principle #5: The Fifth Stone

Everything is responsive.

The universe responds to our most sacred intentions.

Primal Alignment: Pray and Create

We learn to be clear.

We learn to engage the world with embodied prayer.

We serve the unseen world by bringing beauty into the world.

The Dreamer's Questions:

What am I to do?

How am I to move the blocked energy and reestablish

sacred relationship?

What intentions of mine is the universe currently

responding to?

How do I bridge waking and dreaming?

Shamanic Practice:

Dream-Weaving

CHAPTER 8

Dream-Weaving: Manifesting Change through Prayer

*In practice being a shaman or a mystic is about living
the principles of your spiritual path every day in
your humble way, not running to exotic places in search
of unusual experiences. It is not the Hollywood
moment, but the state of being during rush hour
traffic or after spending hours with a crying child or
when you've just burnt the last piece of toast.
It is about not only recognizing the miraculous
in the seemingly mundane, but experiencing
the miraculousness of the mundane.*

Joan Parisi Wilcox,
*Keepers of the Ancient Knowledge:
The Mystical World of the Q'ero Indians of Peru*

EVERYTHING YOU SAY IS A PRAYER! Everything you think is a prayer!
Everything you do is a prayer! The universe answers every prayer.
So what are you praying for right now?

The notion that the universe is responsive is both liberating and frightening. If we understand that the world is alive, conscious, dynamic, and connected without understanding that it responds to us, this understanding is largely meaningless as a guide to living. As with the questions we learned to ask of our dreams, we come now to the place where we ask, "What am I to do? How am I to act in the world?"

We can't continue to act as if the world was filled with unconscious, inanimate stuff for us to use or abuse, consume, defile, or hoard without consequence. For all our technological advances, we know that there is no maturity, depth, or soul in the materialist dream we have been living. We also know that we are squandering our children's natural inheritance, if not living on borrowed time ourselves. We can't continue to live the fundamentalist conservative dream that things won't change. When we see the true nature of things, we know it is foolish to place ourselves in opposition to that nature. We cannot continue to pretend that what we choose to do has no bearing on anyone or anything else and that community is some quaint, archaic, and irrelevant idea. If we have material abundance and our neighbors are wanting, we can spend our money building higher walls and paying for higher and higher levels of violence to defend our possessions, or we can ensure that those around us are not wanting for the basic necessities of life.

How, then, are we to live in a world that is alive, conscious, dynamic, connected, and, above all, responsive? My answer to that, the one best answer I have learned from shamans, medicine carriers, and healers, is deceptively simple: We are to live prayerfully, in gratitude and sacred reciprocity.

But does that mean we are to remain passive, receiving whatever the universe has to offer? Are we to pray and make offerings, then sit back and wait? Some spiritual paths would seem to suggest that we are. We are told that all we need to do is visualize our way to health and happiness. We are told that our negative thought patterns have caused our disease and misfortune, and that if we just focus on love and light, everything will be fine. Set an intention and see it how you want it to be, and Spirit will make it so.

I don't believe it works that way, and I don't believe our Stone Age ancestors could afford to act that way. Our ancestors had no qualms about acting in the world. They didn't wait around for dinner to walk up and die in front of them. They knew they had to take an active role in engaging the universe, but they did it prayerfully and with attention to the sacred. They knew that the universe would provide for them, but only if they made the right choices regarding both the spirit and the physical worlds. They made certain that they were aligned with the natural world and the spirit world first. They lived each day in relationship to a sacred unseen world. They struggled to walk in beauty and do the right thing according to Spirit. They attended to the messages of their dreams and they sought visionary experiences to ensure that they were living in balance and alignment.

Before they hunted, they asked for guidance, permission, and assistance. Perhaps they journeyed to the master or mistress of the animals to ask for a successful hunt. Their shaman might have shape-shifted into the form of their prey, allowing the hunters to symbolically kill him. There might have been a ritual to bless the hunters and thank the prey in advance. But then, after all that preparation, they still needed to go out and hunt their prey in the physical world. If they did not actually hunt, Spirit had no channel through which to respond to their request.

There is a teaching story that goes like this:

> *A man is praying to God to save him from the rising floodwaters of a river. He is interrupted once by a man with a truck offering to drive him to higher ground. "No thanks," he replies. "God will protect me."*
>
> *As the floodwaters rise, he is forced to the second floor of his house and still he prays fervently. Once again he is interrupted, but this time by a man with a boat offering to rescue him. "No thanks," he replies again. "I'm sure God will answer my prayers."*
>
> *Finally the floodwaters force him onto his roof, where he prays that much harder. This time a helicopter lowers a ladder down, but he refuses to climb up it. "I'll be fine," he shouts up at the pilot. "God will take care of me."*
>
> *The floodwaters continue to rise, submerging the house and, finally, drowning the man. When he arrives in heaven he asks God what happened. "I prayed for your salvation, but you ignored my prayers," the man says bitterly.*
>
> *"What do you mean I ignored your prayers?" God replies. "I sent you a man with a truck, a man with a boat, and a man with a helicopter, and each time you refused my help."*

It is vitally important that we acknowledge the unseen world, but that is not, in itself, enough. We need to open channels by which Spirit can reach us and answer our prayers. We are meant to participate in the creation of our world. This participation is a kind of dream-weaving.

Marcus Braybrooke writes in the book *Learn to Pray: A Practical Guide to Faith and Inspiration,* "When you ask in prayer, you have to act in support of your asking...Commitment to action is an integral part of your prayer. Prayer gives you access to the divine, which brings you untold strength. But the matter cannot be surrendered from your hands."

Dream-weaving requires vigilance. We must constantly be aware of how we are praying and what we are praying for in word, thought, and action. The Aborigines of Australia sing their world into existence on a regular basis. If a line from the song is lost, that part of the world may return to the Dreaming. John Perkins, shamanic teacher and founder of the Dream Change Coalition, writes, "The world is as you dream it." The universe gives us the world we dream. If we want a different world, we need to dream a different dream. We can only dream a new dream when our words, our thoughts, and our actions are aligned and congruent. We can only dream-weave as conscious co-creators of our world when our prayers are given form through creativity, right action, and the willingness to live our personal power. Remember that the shamanic path is not the mystic's path. It is not about observing from the mountaintop and removing oneself from all temptations. It is about fully living your life as both a human being having a spiritual experience and a spiritual being having a human experience.

When we consecrate ground by creating a cross within a circle, we deliberately draw Spirit (from the north) down into physical form (in the south). In *The Soul's Code,* James Hillman writes that from birth, from the time our soul incarnates, our struggle is not to grow up but to "grow down" into who we were meant to be. We don't grow down by waiting and wishing and hoping for the best. We grow down by engaging the world with the courage of our creative daimon, seeking right action according to spiritual guidance, and refusing to be less than we are.

What Are You Praying For?

Spoken Prayers

The common view of prayer is that it is a discrete action that we turn on and off, as if God can only hear us when we pick up the special prayer telephone. This has always seemed to me to paint God (and I'm using the word God here to denote Great Spirit, the universal life force, or whatever overarching deity of whatever gender best suits you) rather simplistically. The shaman would say that while dedicated prayer does concentrate and focus energy, God hears everything we think and say and do as being our true prayers. God is the ultimate shaman, able to pick up our double signals in prayers. He does not answer the pious prayers on Sunday when the real prayers that have been thought and spoken and lived during the week conflict so significantly. Our true prayers are answered. We get the world we are dreaming—the world we are praying for by our thoughts, words, and actions. It would behoove us, therefore, to be very clear about what we are thinking, giving voice to, and enacting.

◈ STONE AGE WISDOM PRACTICE #22:

Carrying the Turtle Stone

One of the things I ask my students to do is go on a negativity fast. I don't believe that it is ever very successful to simply tell people to think differently, but I do want my students to become aware of their thoughts. Instead, I focus on what they are giving voice to—how they are praying by what they say.

1. Find a smooth, rounded river stone about the size of a flattened grapefruit. It is important that it be large and obvious, not a pocket stone. Wash and dry your stone and consider cleansing it with sage smoke, as described on page 220.

2. Select three days after the new moon and before the full moon. During those three days, you must carry the stone wherever you go. It must always be within reach. That means that even when you are home, it must travel from room to room with you (yes, that includes the bathroom). You must carry it into business meetings with you. It must travel with you in the car, bus, or plane.

3. For the three days of your negativity fast, you're simply to avoid giving voice to negative thoughts. You may think them as much as you want, but you must refrain from saying anything negative, critical, disparaging, judgmental, or mean.

When you find these thoughts entering your head and you are tempted to give voice to them, touch your stone. Allow the stone to help you avoid those dark and heavy prayers. In Peru, dark, dense, heavy energy is called *jucha*. There is no negative connotation to the concept of jucha, it is simply considered to be unhealthy for humans to carry around. We might think of it like carbon dioxide. Trees need it, but we can't breathe it. We give them our exhalations (carbon dioxide) and they give us their exhalations (oxygen). In the same way, we feed our jucha (our heavy, dense energy) to the Earth Mother. She transforms it and returns it to us in ways that sustain us.

4. If you find that you slip too many times, add more time to your negativity fast. Remember that you are not trying to control your thoughts, just your expression of those thoughts. Carrying the stone is a physical reminder of what you are attempting (especially when you have to explain to people why you are carrying this stone).

5. After the third day, bury the stone in the Earth for 24 hours to discharge these heavy prayers. As you are burying it, think about how much you had to use the stone. These negative or

heavy thoughts are your actual prayers. They are your double-signal prayers. What have you been praying for?

6. Dig up and clean off the stone. Carry it periodically when you feel yourself slipping back into the place of expressing your dark prayers.

The negativity fast is not meant to cure you of "negative" emotions. It is not even meant to cure you of expressing them. Rather it is meant to call your attention to your patterns and your double signals. If you aspire to be a pillar of spiritual light, perhaps like your favorite guru, but you constantly express anger and judgment, you are lacking congruence and the full weight of your personal power is not aligned with your soul purpose.

"Negative" emotions are an important part of your existence. They are the voice of your soul as surely as any other message you might receive. If you experience anger and fear and envy, these feelings are telling you something. To learn from them it is imperative that we embrace them, move more deeply into them, and give them a voice. We do not have to act on them or wallow in them or be directed by them, but we must bring them into our conscious awareness. The negativity fast is a way of becoming more conscious.

Remember that speech is powerful. Your choice of words *does* matter. Your words can curse or bless. Imagine your own spirit guide following you around on any given day and keeping track of the number of blessings and the number of curses you bestow. What would your tally look like at the end of the day?

If the idea of blessing someone or something spontaneously seems uncomfortable, consider memorizing a blessing that appeals to you. There are many different simple blessings from many different cultures. When I was working on my book *The Artist Inside: A Spiritual Guide to Cultivating Your Creative Self,* I received this blessing from a spirit guide during a shamanic journey:

> *May you travel deep and true in the Dreaming.*
> *May you travel with healing power and courage, wisdom*
> *and enchantment.*
> *May the spirits guide your going and guard your safe return.*

This is an elemental Gaelic blessing:
> *Deep peace of the running wave be upon you*
> *Deep peace of the flowing air be upon you*
> *Deep peace of the quiet earth be upon you*
> *Deep peace of the shining stars be upon you*

This is a Navajo blessing:
> *May you walk in beauty,*
> *Beauty beside you,*
> *Beauty before you,*
> *Beauty behind you,*
> *Beauty above you,*
> *Beauty beneath you,*
> *Beauty within you,*
> *May you walk the beauty way.*

Are you comfortable praying out loud? As you become more aware of the prayers you are unconsciously giving voice to, you might consider using your voice to pray consciously. My friend and fellow shamanic practitioner Carl Hyatt shared how he learned to pray out loud. Once a week, he and a friend met at dawn by the ocean. They walked out among the stones of the rocky New England shore and built little stone cairns. As they piled the stones atop each other, they expressed prayers of gratitude to the Earth, the ocean, the sky, and the fish. They overcame their embarrassment by continuing their litany for as long as they could. Every natural occurrence, from the cry of a seagull to the movement of a cloud to the crashing of a wave was woven into the prayer as an ongoing dialogue of gratitude.

Thought Prayers

There is another kind of unconscious praying we engage in—these are the prayers embedded in the stories we tell about ourselves. As a shamanic counselor, one of my jobs is to listen. By the time some people come to me, they have often exhausted many of the contemporary Western modes of healing, both physical and psychological. These are not ignorant people. They often have advanced degrees and are well respected in their fields. They come to me with stories—stories of pain, sorrow, disillusionment, disappointment, betrayal, and frustration. They also come to me with hidden stories. In these hidden stories, they are the hero and the main character. It is these stories I have learned to listen for. The stories they are currently living reflect the archetypal energy field in which they are playing, and the role within that field is usually the place they are stuck. By stuck, I simply mean that a given role within a field allows for only a limited palette of responses, and those responses may no longer be serving the individual well.

Your story is how you define yourself. It is who you think you are. Your story may relate to your job, but it doesn't have to. A woman's story might actually be "the good mother," even though she is a lawyer, doctor, or businesswoman. A story, especially an archetypal one, carries with it certain expectations. We would not be satisfied with our masculine warrior stories if at the end the foe was not completely vanquished. We would be equally shocked if the good mother resolved a conflict between her two children by killing one of them. The warrior is supposed to triumph by skill and force and the ability to discern right from wrong. The good mother is supposed to triumph through compassion, self-sacrifice, and caretaking. Embedded within the warrior's story are prayers that begin, "Let me win," because the warrior knows that winning is how he will be judged. Embedded within the mother's story are prayers that begin, "Let them like me," because the mother knows that being nice and being liked is how the mother is judged. I've used the masculine and the feminine pronouns here because these stories traditionally are played out by warrior men and mothering women, but it doesn't have to be that way. With today's shifting roles, these stories could be played out by men or women.

There is nothing wrong with either story (or any of the other possible archetypal stories) as long as your story serves you. Unfortunately, most of us stay stuck in story patterns long past when they have ceased serving us. We lack the elders and the storytellers who might make us aware of our particular stories and what the appropriate new ones might be. We also lack the series of culturally recognized rites of passage that were once designed to move us from story to story.

We need a deep understanding of the power behind the stories we tell. We tell stories about our lives. We accept or reject stories about our place in the world. In the end, however, our lives and our world can be no better than the stories we tell. Telling stories is at once personal and communal. Myth making is the soul's poetry. Part of dream-weaving is looking at the important events of our lives, both joyous and traumatic, as if they were the working out of our unique destiny—our soul's calling. Every pivotal moment reflects some adjustment or accommodation between our own unique essence or daimon and the life we are living. Retelling our personal stories as if every dramatic moment moved us forward in some way may not make any moment less painful, but it does give us a context in which the pain of loss, separation, failure, and illness has meaning.

A woman comes to me with stories of childhood abuse, failed relationships, abandonment, and life-threatening illness. Still, her dreams call her to heal herself and to heal others. In choosing to accept this path of service, she agrees to look at her stories from a fresh perspective. She explores myths and stories of shamanic initiation from cultures around the world. Some are the antecedents of our classic fairy tales. She agrees to rewrite her life story as a fairy tale—one in which she is the heroine, tested again and again, transformed in the refining fire of life. She shares her story in a ceremony of rebirth, witnessed by a circle of friends. All at once she is at a new threshold. Stepping forward from a place of power, she can choose to engage life by remaining in alignment with and sacred relationship to Spirit, asking for what she wants and creating ways for Spirit to fulfill her request. This is a process that is open to anyone.

◈ STONE AGE WISDOM PRACTICE #23:

Finding a New Story

I've come to believe that there are several important things that need to happen if we are to avoid being stuck in our stories, redreaming a toxic dream over and over again, praying unconsciously for exactly the life we don't want.

To begin, we need to have the personal stories we are currently carrying heard by others. Some of us have felt so unheard, so unnoticed, or so unloved that our stories take on a huge significance in our lives. If you believe your story is not a story, it only means that it has taken on such a huge significance in your life or that you've become so attached to it that you cannot see around its edges. It's as if you're sitting in the front row of a movie theater with so much of your peripheral vision filled with imagery that you forget you're watching a movie. If you've forgotten your story is just a story, the only way out of the trap is to have your story heard and witnessed. Your family probably can't do it, but that isn't their fault. They were never meant to. Compassionate circles can hear your story. Therapeutic groups can hear your story. Twelve Step programs have been successful because they have witnessed the stories of their members. The only thing to be wary of is a group that hears your story only to keep you in that story. This sometimes happens in well-meaning groups founded to support issues of victimization. If hearing your story is a step in the process, that's fine. If the story you find yourself telling brings you power or status in the group, it will be hard to let go of.

Once our story is told, we need to pull back from the personal details of our story to see the pattern that is being enacted. Dreams are a great way to do this. Exploring a dream according to the guiding questions described in chapter 3 (see page 79) will help you see your current life pattern clearly. Again, this can sometimes be difficult to do. It is hard to see the dreamspirit that looks like your mother in your dreams as anything other than your mother. To see the energetic or archetypal quality of the dream, you have to understand that "the mother" in the dream is both a symbol for a kind of energy and a living energy that is separate and distinct from "your mother."

Another way of becoming aware of the archetypal quality of your own story is to explore myths and fairytales. See yourself in the role of the main character and recast the events of your life as elements in the story. For my students, I share some of the archetypal stories of the shamanic calling and initiation. These stories are tales of descent, misfortune, and dismemberment. But these hardships have meaning. They have a purpose in moving the individual into alignment with a soul calling to be of healing service. They accomplish what James Hillman calls for in his book *The Soul's Code: In Search of Character and Calling*. Hillman is hoping that this exploration of your soul story will "resurrect the unaccountable twists that turned your boat around in the eddies and shallows of meaninglessness, bringing you back to feelings of destiny...."

Once your current story has been acknowledged and heard, you can release your attachment to it. You can see your story as a dream—as an energetic or archetypal story—to see where and how it no longer serves you. You might want to create a ritual to give form to your desire to release that story. But whether you do this or not, you become free to re-imagine your story. We tend to view our lives at any give moment as being the last few pages of a novel. We're constantly disappointed that the story does not seem to end with any resolution or to even make sense. We can look back at things that happened 20 years ago and understand why they were necessary to the plot and the hero's journey, but if we assume we are on the last pages, the things currently happening to us seem to make no sense.

Try rewriting your life story over a different template. One that recognizes that there was a calling—a reason for your being born— and that aligns with that calling, accepting that every accident, mishap, and difficult moment has been an essential part of the story. This new story moves you out of blame or guilt without requiring forgiveness. We do not need to forgive the people who have hurt us in order to stop blaming them. We can realize that there were people and events that we needed to experience if we were to live out our calling.

If I've made the idea of becoming conscious of your old story and adopting a new one sound intriguing, I've succeeded. If I've made it sound easy, I've overshot my mark. We cling to our stories. We hold tightly to them because no matter how dysfunctional and crippling they are, they are the devil we know. It takes courage and perseverance to release an old story pattern. You need courage to face the unknown and perseverance to hold onto the new story long enough for the people around you to stop complaining and accept your new story.

Embodied Prayers

If you've examined the unconscious prayers to which you've been giving voice and the thought prayers connected to your old story patterns, it shouldn't be difficult to find the ways you've been unconsciously praying by action. So let's shift out of what we are doing that no longer serves us and into practices that might serve us better.

When you give physical form to a prayer, you embody it. Aligning thought, speech, and action behind a prayer amplifies the prayer's energy. The simplest forms of prayer are often expressions of gratitude. Navajo medicine carriers often greet the sunrise with a prayer and a pinch of corn pollen as an offering. The Q'ero of the Andes splash a little liquid from a cup or bottle onto the ground before drinking—the first drink is always for Pachamama—the Earth Mother. Christians say a prayer of grace and gratitude before eating a meal. Tibetan Buddhists and Muslims prostrate themselves on the ground in prayer and devotion. The Lakota smoke a pinch of tobacco in a sacred pipe to pray.

How might you weave embodied prayers into your day? Here are a few suggestions.

• Greet the new day by stepping outside and facing the direction of the rising sun. Offer a pinch of tobacco or cornmeal to the earth, and express your gratitude for another day.

• Light a stick of incense on your altar in the morning and sit in prayer until it has burned down.

• Bless your food by holding your hands over it and radiating it with healthy, life-giving energy. Say a prayer of gratitude to the Earth for providing your sustenance.

• Make a meeting space sacred at work by arranging symbols of the elements on a conference table or side table. You might include flowers, stones, crystals, a bowl of water with a few drops of essential oil in it, a feather, a candle, and some symbol representing a prayer for the success of the project. One of the things I have done at corporate meetings is provide a small, tumbled, semiprecious stone for each participant. I add a little card explaining the spiritual or energetic significance of the stone. It is an unusual way to start a meeting—everyone sharing the meaning of his or her stone—but it definitely shifts the energy in a positive direction. Even the people who claim to have no interest in such "New Age" or spiritual things can't help picking up their stones and holding them at different times during the meeting.

• In the middle of even the most frustrating day, take a moment to walk outside and make an offering to the Earth (tobacco, cornmeal, coffee, spring water, whatever you have).

Express gratitude for something you have, and feel how rejuvenated you feel.

• Give a homeless person some change, but make it a prayer of gratitude. Put money in a donation jar, but make it a prayer of thanks. Do someone a kindness without expecting anything in return. Make a habit out of it.

You can also embody your prayers in more formal ways.

• Make tobacco prayer ties by placing pinches of tobacco into small squares of red cloth and tying them off with red string. Pray as you tie, sending your prayers into each bundle. How many bundles should you tie? How important is your prayer? Tie all of the bundles to one long line of red string. Find a tree you can decorate with your prayer ties. Repeat the prayer again as you hang each bundle over a branch, then walk away.

• Write your prayers on strips of paper. Tie each strip around a found stick of dry wood. Build a fire and slowly add your prayer sticks to the fire one at a time. Don't add another stick until the previous one has been consumed. Let the smoke carry your prayers.

• Buy a good bottle of wine and place it on your altar. Every time you sit at your altar to pray, tie a thread around the bottle. After a month or two, when the bottle is well-tied with your prayer threads, invite a friend or friends to help you drink the wine. Before drinking the wine, cut the threads and bury them in the Earth. Splash a little of the wine over the buried threads before pouring any to drink. Drink the wine slowly and reverently.

An even more formal process for embodying prayers is the despacho or Earth offering tradition from Peru. (See page 246.)

Despachos and Earth Offerings

One of the most beautiful forms of an embodied prayer is the Peruvian tradition of the despacho. The despacho is an offering. In material terms, it is a kind of natural mandala made from flowers, candy, colored paper, seeds, beans, string, food, things that shine and glitter, and man-made and naturally found objects laid out on a piece of paper. The paper is then folded, tied with string, and either burned or buried. In spiritual terms, a despacho is a prayer, a request, an expression of gratitude, and a ritual feeding of the spirits of Earth and mountain. In Peru it is possible to walk into a market and purchase a despacho kit for healing, encouraging good fortune, or attracting love, to name just a few of the many options.

You can create a despacho as an embodied prayer with items that are common to your area. Despachos lend a natural focus to group rituals. The despacho can hold the individual prayers of a collective (the analogy being a single envelope with a lot of different prayers) or it can carry one group prayer. Despachos can be done with specific requests in mind or on behalf of individuals needing healing, or they can be done as simple offerings. What I describe below is not the traditional Peruvian way of creating despachos, nor does my despacho utilize the traditional ingredients of a despacho. I believe that what matters most is your heartfelt intention and the activation of your own creative connection to the divine. (For information about more traditional despachos, see "Resources" on page 266.)

1. To begin, identify the purpose or the intention of the despacho. Ask for what you want with confidence. Don't make foolish or half-hearted requests. The phrase "Be careful what you wish

for" comes to mind here. Think about all the ways your life might be different if you really got what you were praying for. Are you ready for that? Be vigilant about where the request is coming from. Is it originating from your daimon or your soul's mission? Your commitment and your desire are the driving forces behind your prayer. Write down your request in simple language. As you assemble the despacho, continually repeat the request as a prayer.

2. Find a large sheet of paper on which to lay out the despacho ingredients. This piece of paper will end up being folded, tied, and burned. I suggest white paper, but use what calls to you. You will also need some red or white string to tie the despacho. Smudge the paper you will use with sage or sweetgrass smoke.

3. Begin by laying your written request in the center of the piece of paper. If the despacho will hold many different requests, these can be added later. On top of your request, lay a small scallop shell with the bowl facing up and the scalloped edge facing away from you. This symbolizes the Earth Mother, the ocean, and the divine feminine. On top of the shell, place a small cross to represent the Creator Spirit, the sky, and the divine masculine.

4. Add three-leaf clusters of leaves (known as *kintus* in Peru). These can be from a local indigenous plant or they can be dried bay or olive leaves. Join the kintus and blow your prayer request into each cluster three times to symbolize the three worlds and the three energies. You may place any number of kintus that speaks to you. You might want to place a kintu for the four cardinal directions as well as for above, below, and within. If another number has significance for the request, add that many kintus. Arrange them in a pleasing pattern on the paper.

5. The traditional rationale for the offering included in a despacho is that certain spirits that have dominion over certain kinds of

issues in life like certain kinds of food. The Tirakuna in the south, who have dominion over physical healing, prefer animal products (fur, fat, bone, meat, butter, claws, and so on). The Auquis in the west, who heal emotional issues, prefer plant products (leaves, seeds, grasses, fruits, beans, and vegetables). The Malquis in the north, who heal spiritual issues, prefer mineral products (small stones, crystals, magnetic ore, and sand). The Machukuna in the east, who heal mental and psychological issues, prefer objects that are human-made (metal figurines, cut paper figures, woven fabric, and toys). In addition to this, you may want to consider brightly colored candies, glitter, gold and silver foil pieces, colored threads, cotton balls, and a little wine or alcohol. Be creative in your choice of things to offer. Arrange the objects to please your senses. Every despacho will be different and should reflect the intention of the despacho. For instance, a despacho for a physical healing may have more animal products for the Tirakuna, while a despacho for financial abundance might contain coins or paper money.

6. The ingredients should be separated out in advance in little paper packets. These can sit together or held on each individual's personal altar. One person can arrange the ingredients on the despacho (selecting more or less of any ingredient as he or she is called), or the despacho can be a group project, with each individual arranging their chosen ingredients. After the despacho is complete, lay red or white carnation blossoms on top. Allow the process to unfold according to its own rhythm. Don't rush it. When everything is done, fold the paper into a packet so that nothing will leak out. (There are many ideas about the correct way to do this, but I believe you should worry less about form and trust your intuition.) Tie the packet with red or white string and let it sit on an altar or Mesa until it is ready to be burned or buried.

7. Traditionally, burning a despacho carries prayers up to heaven or up to the spirits of the mountain peaks (called Apus). Burying a despacho feeds the Earth Mother (Pachamama). Burning a despacho usually feels more satisfying, but again, trust your instincts. Remember to sing, chant, or speak as you burn your despacho to give voice to your embodied prayer.

A despacho is a very specific form of embodied prayer. There is another way that we dream-weave and pray in embodied forms, and that is by engaging in the sacred creative cycle.

Deep in our ancestral memory lies a connection between artistic expression and Spirit. The native and indigenous cultures from which we've all descended understood this connection. In fact, the idea that art could somehow be separated from the sacred is only a rather recent idea. For tribal peoples today, the "work" of art is the manifestation of Spirit in material form. When an Aborigine engages in artistic expression, he first accesses the realm of Spirit, seeking what we might call inspiration or the breath of the divine. This divine inspiration is then translated into material form with words, images, music, dance, or artifacts. Now that the spirit has been seduced into material form, we can engage with it in ritual. This ritual releases that spirit and draws artist and community alike back into sacred communion with the divine, thus completing the cycle. This is the sacred creative cycle. It is a cycle of transformation. When art is about transformation, it is a sacred practice.

Engaging the sacred creative cycle is one of the primary ways we can connect with Spirit in our lives. How do you express your divine creative energy? Do you write poetry or prose? Do you paint, sculpt, or photograph? Do you cook, garden, or sew? Do you act, dance, sing, or play an instrument? Do you bring beauty into the world? Creating is praying in embodied form.

But creating is also more than that. I'll go out on a limb here and say that if you aren't expressing yourself creatively in the world, you are not whole. The feeling that something is wrong with your life might simply be the result of not living a creative life. The shamans that I have met have invariably also been artists or craftspeople. They make beautiful things; they pray in physical form. They create what the Siberian shamans call *ongons,* or spirit houses. They paint with acrylics or oils, or with sand, tiny seed beads, or colorful yarn pressed into beeswax. They decorate drums and staves and medicine bags. They weave beautiful fabrics. They create wands and mandalas. They pray in poetic verses and they weave stories that are magical.

Most of us get as hung up on the idea of being an artist as we would about being a shaman. Remember that the world cannot have too many shamans with a small "s." It also cannot have too many artists with a small "a." Do you collect things (especially if you collect things with no consideration of their investment value)? If so, you may be the artist as hunter. Hunters have courage and patience and stamina. They attend to their environment. You walk softly and silently, journal in hand, through the jungles of your next yard sale or flea market. Whenever you dream of an object, an animal, a character, or a place in a strong and clear way, or in several dreams in a row, it shows up in your waking life. Your job as a finder is to leave yourself open to the possibility of finding your dreams already in physical form in the waking world. You might stalk your dreamspirits with a camera, sketchbook, or collecting bag, but you know they are out there.

Do you like to organize things into visually pleasing arrangements? Arrangers are altar builders. You may not call your arrangement an altar or shrine, but you create sacred space all the same. An altar can be as simple as river stones arranged in careful order on a shelf or as complex as a corner of a room draped with photographs, fabric, vessels, found objects, dolls, gifts, and religious icons. You may have even been creating altars without realizing it. The act of conscious altar building, however, increases the power of the altars you build. When you make an altar, think of yourself as a teacher. One of the most important functions a teacher serves is that he or she creates a space where learning—an exchange of information or energy—can occur. An arranger is a space artist. Imagine your home filled with special places for your collections—tabletops, shelves, cabinets. Imagine cleaning, shifting, and rearranging your altars to reflect your journeys into dreamtime.

Do you like to alter and combine things in new and imaginative ways? If you create by altering, think of yourself as a healer. You take what comes to you and shift its energy. This is a subtle process. You vision-shift to get inside the object you find. You merge with it, feeling as it feels, sensing as it senses. You listen with compassion and nonattachment. When you understand what will build and strengthen the energy of this object, you act upon it. You might bind together two objects as carefully and meticulously as a doctor setting a bone or a surgeon grafting skin. You might mark a stone or shell with paint, ink, or metallic leaf. You might press a design into a piece of wet clay. You might wrap a leaf around a bone and tie it with braided grass twine. Each action, each alteration strengthens, shifts, or forges a new energetic connection.

Do you paint, sculpt, or otherwise create something out of nothing but raw materials? Those who make imagery or artifacts are artists as magicians. Perhaps you paint magic mandalas on canvas, filling in the painting with the colors from your shamanic journeys. Or maybe you shape-shift into bear to breathe life into a little ceramic figure, or into spider to weave or embroider an altar cloth that maps your journeys, or into beaver to throw spirit vessels of mud and clay on a potter's wheel.

Nicholas Wood has written a beautiful book about shamanism with an emphasis on sacred objects, their creation, and their use. In *Voices from the Earth: Practical Shamanism*, he writes, "You are part of the dance that is the creation of sacred craftwork and you are unique. What speaks to you will become a part of the language you develop and use. What you make is real. Your language is true for you. Be true to it."

Engagement and Detachment

You can't always get what you want.
But if you try sometime, you just might find,
You get what you need.

Mick Jagger

Prayer, even embodied prayer, does not guarantee that we will get everything we want when we want it. In fact, I'm pretty sure that the way prayer works is that you can either specify *what* you want to happen or *when* you want something to happen, but not both. This is where detachment comes in.

I know that there is a god or goddess or universal force that responds to my prayers, but I'm also aware that this force knows far more about my purpose and mission here than I will ever know. When I pray, I gather my energy behind my request. I try to be clear and congruent. I ask if I'm sending any double signals. I embody my prayer in ritual and creative form, and then I release it. I once heard someone describe a prayer as a thought-form rocket into the future. Well, once I've launched that rocket, I detach from the outcome. I don't mean to sound flip about this, but I try to imagine what I would want if I were the goddess in charge of answering prayers. I sure wouldn't want to be nagged. "Could you hurry it up?" "Nothing seems to be happening yet." "Remember me? I prayed for something just last week."

I think that what I'm supposed to do after I put that prayer out into the world is act as though it were going to be answered affirmatively and begin doing the practical work to be ready for it. Once I've prayed, I hold space for the vision of that prayer being answered with objects on my Mesa or images on my wall, but I also begin opening channels. If I pray to meet someone, it is my responsibility to go to places where there are people. If I need money, it is my task to arrange for the universe to send me money.

Sometimes I get what I want after I've forgotten I had asked for it. Sometimes I get something different than I asked for. I have to trust this process in both cases.

Dream-weaving is also about living life according to the shamanic worldview. As I was completing this book, I made a journey back to Gray Morning Bear. I found him on the precipice of a high, stony mountain. He had built a small fire and his bearskin blanket was wrapped around his shoulders. He was rattling and singing as I sat quietly and respectfully across the fire from him. I became aware that I had a pouch slung over my shoulder, and I knew that I had the pages of my manuscript inside.

After I had heard Gray Morning Bear's plaintive song enough times to have memorized it, he stopped abruptly and looked up at me, as if noticing me for the first time. He laughed as he looked down at my pouch. I looked down to see a beautiful black and tan spider perched atop the bag.

"So, Grandmother Spider's medicine is in there now?" he asked.

"I don't know," I answered honestly. "I tried to be true to what you taught me, but it's only a book. I'm not sure that any of Grandmother Spider's medicine will come through a book."

"Do you believe the words that are in that bag?"

"Yes." I swallowed hard. I did believe them. I had been teaching them, struggling to live them, trying to translate them for the time I lived in.

"Then stop feeling sorry for yourself," he growled. "Let's pray on it." He extended his hand and I handed him the pouch carefully. The spider crawled from the pouch onto Gray Morning Bear's arm, and then up to his shoulder. There she sat staring at me, as if withholding judgment. He pulled a handful of sage leaves from a hide bag by his feet and tossed them onto the fire. Then he pulled the manuscript of loose pages from my pouch. He sniffed the pages and listened to the sound they made fluttering in the wind. I wondered if he could hear the words I had written. He held the manuscript over the aromatic smoke that was now rising from the fire. After a long pause he spoke.

"These are good words," he said solemnly. "Let's see if anyone will hear them." With that, he tossed the pages high up into the air. My stomach sank. I knew I was journeying. I knew that somewhere back on the other side of the Dreaming, my manuscript was safe. But still I felt nauseous.

Time seemed to slow down. I could feel the wind wanting to take the pages, starting to peel back the leaves to scatter and shuffle them all over the valley below. At the same time I was aware of a sharp cry overhead. I could see the pages beginning to separate. I felt the cold wind snap.

Then the eagle was there, snatching up the manuscript in sharp talons, before a single page could get away. We watched as the eagle soared out over the valley, riding the thermal currents in great spirals. We watched and watched until there was nothing left to see, and still we watched a little longer.

"Aho," he said.

"Aho," I agreed.

"So you've made your prayer. It was a good one. Now walk away."

He smiled at me and I knew he was right. It was time to let this prayer go.

Urban Contemporary Shamanism

*In the modern world, the techniques that
were evolved by traditional shamans to heighten
their consciousness can be used to explore
and discover your own place in the universe.
By following their path, you can come to see more
clearly how you are enmeshed in the whole of creation.*

Will Adcock,
*Dream Wisdom and Shamanism:
Spiritual Journeying for Greater Inner Knowledge*

I WROTE THIS BOOK WITH THE HOPE that more people might find a way to live according to the worldview of our Stone Age ancestors, existing hunter-gatherer tribes, and of contemporary shamanic practitioners. I know that books and workshops don't make shamans, but I hope that this may serve as a catalyst for people seeking an earth-centered spirituality based on sacred relationship.

I must confess, however, that the distinction I've been making between shamanic healers and those seeking a personal spiritual practice based on shamanism is specious. If you begin to live by the principles of Grandmother Spider's Five Stones, you will not just be serving yourself. You will be serving Spirit, serving your community, serving the planet, and serving the magical living universe. You may also find yourself called to heal others in the true sense of helping them move toward wholeness in their lives. This is important work. Sarangerel, the author of *Riding Windhorses: A Journey into the Heart of Mongolian Shamanism*, writes, "Why is shamanism so important to world culture? The simplest answer is that it espouses a view of the world that is vital to humanity's future survival."

If this book serves its purpose, if the vision of this book grows corn, if the prayer of this book is answered, you may want to learn more about shamanism. You may hear in the crisis of your life the call to heal. You may be drawn into the world and the practice of the urban contemporary shaman. To that end, I'd like to say something about what is happening in the transformation and evolution of planetary shamanism.

As we move into the third millennium, a new, modern form of shamanism seems to be evolving. Traditional shamanism is usually categorized as being "foreign," "other," and "authentic." The new, modern category, however, includes a broad range of practices, from secularized traditional practices to New Age, self-help applications. Gini Graham Scott writes in *The Complete Idiot's Guide to Shamanism*,

> *Some of the major ways in which modern shamanism has changed from traditional shamanism and is likely to keep changing are these:*

• *More syncretism based on the blending of many influences*
• *More individual use for self-development and self-healing*
• *More secularization, in taking shamanism out of a religious or spiritual context, so it is turned into a self-help practice, used for pragmatic ends*
• *More use for personal and professional purposes*

At first these differences seem valid, but the more I think about them, the more I question them. First of all, shamanic practices have always been syncretic. Shamans and their practices have survived precisely because, without the burden of dogma and religious tenets, they have been free to adopt new techniques. Will this process continue and increase with the spread of Western urban culture and the technologies of communication and exchange? Undoubtedly, but this is a difference in degree, not a fundamental difference in how shamanism is practiced.

Second, while I agree that much of shamanism in the New Age community seems to be about self-development and self-help, most traditional shamans come to the practice through a need for personal healing. Lengthy apprenticeships are actually a process of self-development and self-healing.

Scott's third point, that secularization will increase, is both true and problematic, if you define religion and spirituality as most people do. Michael Harner's school of thought, Core Shamanism, has made a specific point of secularizing the techniques of shamanism, but most of the practitioners I know have adopted a belief system from one tradition or another. Sometimes we find a perfect fit; sometimes we integrate several belief systems. The practice leads us into a place that is both more spiritual and less religious. I think that what is more important than which spiritual tradition we adopt is how deeply we live it. If we believe that the elements of earth, water, air, and fire are significant, do we honor them daily? Do we attend to their meaning in our lives? Do we deeply engage with the movement of energies, the images of dreamtime, and the visionary experiences of waking life? Do we live our cosmology? For many of us, science is the religion of urban contemporary culture. Science is the cosmology or big story we operate within. The way of the urban contemporary shaman may be the integration of science and spirituality.

The final point Scott makes is that modern shamanism will see more use for personal and professional purposes. This seems a bit biased. People have always sought out shamans for personal healing and for professional and pragmatic reasons. How is the farmer who wants to know why his sheep aren't reproducing different from the small business owner who wants to know what is keeping his business from growing? Is a mother who lives in a tiny village so different from a mother who lives in a modern suburban neighborhood, when it comes to being concerned about the health or well-being of her child? It seems to me that what defines shamanism, whether traditional or modern, has more to do with the answers than the questions. If a shaman engages the unseen world—enters deeply into his or her cosmology—to find an answer for the farmer or the CEO, there is very little difference between the traditional and the modern shaman.

Urban contemporary shamanic practitioners such as Richard Whiteley, the author of *The Corporate Shaman: A Business Fable*, and José and Lena Stevens, the authors of *The Power Path: The Shaman's Way to Success in Business and Life*, and Alex Stark, a Feng Shui, Geomancy, and shamanic consultant to business in the

New York area, are working to carry the shamanic worldview into business and corporate communities. The shaman goes where healing is needed, and it seems to me that if we have any hope of returning to a balanced relationship with the unseen world, we cannot do it by escaping to exotic and pristine locations. We must do the work where it is most needed.

I'd like to propose another way of thinking about what is happening to shamanism and shamanic healing in this new millennium. I don't believe that the New Age shamanic phenomenon of self-help and self-development is that different from the traditional shamanic path of the healer. It only seems different when we focus on it as an end point. When we see it as part of a continuum or process, it fits the traditional model well.

There is a classical shamanism. It exists in the textbooks of anthropologists, but it is increasingly difficult to find in our world. I think it is useful to study, not because the techniques are more pure or effective, but because it shows us a way of thinking and interacting with the unseen world that owes more to our hunter-gatherer ancestors than to the culture of farmers.

Most everything else that falls into the category of "shamanic" would have to be described as modern, in the sense that it has been impacted upon and influenced by an industrial and techno-logical culture and worldview. Under this category of modern shamanism, I would make some distinctions based primarily upon one's culture of origin.

An individual coming from a more traditional or indigenous culture is more likely to be exposed to a kind of monocultural shamanism. Someone coming from an urban contemporary culture is more likely to encounter a multicultural approach to shamanism. But what they both share is a kind of healing crisis. This needn't be a dramatic physical illness; sometimes the healing crisis is emotional or psychological. Sometimes this healing crisis is expressed as a nagging dissatisfaction, a feeling of being out of balance, or a longing for connection with something that can't even be expressed. The healing crisis is what causes us to seek out Spirit or the unseen. In Western urban cultures we may find ourselves drawn to workshops on shamanism. The focus of these workshops may be self-healing and self-development, and they may be an end unto themselves. I may go away from one or more of these workshops having learned how to live more in balance with the unseen world—to honor my dreams, to alter my consciousness for personal guidance, to attend to the natural world through prayer and ritual offerings. I don't see this as being so different from the individual who seeks out the traditional healer and learns how to restore balance in his or her life through ritual action. In both cases, Spirit has prompted someone to seek balance.

Beyond this step, most people return to their lives with some techniques for remaining balanced and in reciprocal relationship to the unseen world. They may return to the shaman or shamanic teacher occasionally to make adjustments or deal with other issues, but they are not really called to a path of healing service.

Sometimes, however, an individual will go beyond the first few visits with a shaman or the first few classes with a shamanic teacher and engage in an apprenticeship or extended period of study with the purpose and intention of becoming a healer. The difference here between the traditional and the contemporary path is that on the traditional path, the individual openly acknowledges what he or she is doing. Even if there is fear or reluctance about the outcome, the traditional path makes it clear that beyond a certain point, not answering the call to service will be far worse than the rigors of preparing oneself to be of service.

The contemporary path is a bit more ambiguous. We are allowed to study without having to commit ourselves to service, and the ways we may be of service are more varied. I have known many gifted healers from among my fellow students over the years, and it is not unusual for them to have not openly made any commitment to being of healing service. It is actually quite common to find individuals who have studied with one teacher or a variety of teachers for years before they finally reach the conclusion that they are hiding from their true work by continuing to think of themselves as students. While it is certainly true that some people take a couple of workshops and then hang out a shingle as a shaman, it is far more common for gifted healers to avoid "coming out" under the pretext that there are still things to be learned. I avoided my own calling for years, while I continued to "prepare myself." It was finally at the urging of my teacher that I began to carry my medicine on behalf of Spirit, the community, and individuals. I think that this is the sign of a good teacher. If your teacher encourages students to begin being of service through ceremony, counseling, or healing work after a reasonable amount of preparation, you have a good one. If your teacher sees students who begin to practice on their own as a threat, well....

I believe I will always have things to learn and I will always be a student, but I also believe that as long as I am clear about what I can and cannot do, my first obligation is to serve Spirit.

So the place we come to is that of the neotraditional shaman on the monocultural path and the urban contemporary shaman on the multicultural path. Both shamans weave together classical shamanic techniques with contemporary spiritual and energetic practices. Both function as shamans within their communities.

There is more than just *room* for urban contemporary shamanic practitioners; there is a *need*. It may well be that as we progress into this new millennium there will no longer be a distinction between neotraditional shamans and urban contemporary shamans.

Now put down this book and go for a vision walk.

Stalk a beautiful stone.

Pick it up. Can you feel it breathe?

Hold it to your ear. Can you hear it sing?

It has not always been here. It has not always looked this way.

It was hard work getting to be just the right shape

in just the right spot for you to notice.

It used to be a mountain.

If you are going to take it with you, leave an offering.

Tobacco or cornmeal, a strand of hair, or an eyelash.

If you are going to return it to the Earth,

make it a prayer.

Resources

Rather than provide a list of all the books on shamanism that are on my shelves, I've decided to list those books that I have found particularly useful for understanding what an urban contemporary practice of shamanism might be. With a few exceptions, I have not listed books that are histories or works of research. I think these are important and well worth reading, but I was trying to create a reading list that was directly relevant to the content of this book. There is not a book on this list that I have not read and found very useful.

I consider these books to be primary resources for exploring the different roles of the contemporary shaman.

The Shaman as Artist

Crockett, Tom. *The Artist Inside: A Spiritual Guide to Cultivating Your Creative Self.* New York: Broadway Books, 2000.

Wood, Nicholas. *Voices from the Earth: Practical Shamanism.* New York: Godsfield, 2000.

The Shaman as Consciousness Explorer

De Korne, Jim. *Psychedelic Shamanism: The Cultivation, Preparation and Shamanic Use of Psychotropic Plants.* Port Townsend, WA: Breakout Productions, 1998.

Hoffman, Kay. *The Trance Workbook: Understanding and Using the Power of Altered States.* New York: Sterling Publications, 1999.

Narby, Jeremy. *The Cosmic Serpent: DNA and the Origins of Knowledge.* New York: J. P. Tarcher, 1999.

Pinchbeck, Daniel. *Breaking Open the Head: A Psychedelic Journey into the Heart of Contemporary Shamanism*. New York: Broadway Books, 2002.

The Shaman as Dreamer
Adcock, Will, with Rosalind Powell and Laura J. Watts. *Dream Wisdom and Shamanism: Spiritual Journeying for Greater Inner Knowledge*. New York: Arness Publishing, 2001.

Hillman, James. *Dream Animals*. San Francisco: Chronicle Books, 1997. *Out of print.*

Moss, Robert. *Conscious Dreaming: A Spiritual Path for Everyday Life*. New York: Crown, 1996.

The Shaman as Earth Steward
Abram, David. *The Spell of the Sensuous: Perception and Language in a More-Than-Human World*. New York: Vintage Books, 1997.

Cruden, Loren. *The Spirit of Place: A Workbook for Sacred Alignment*. Rochester, VT: Destiny Books, 1995.

Devereux, Paul. *Re-Visioning the Earth: A Guide to Opening the Healing Channels Between Mind and Nature*. New York: Fireside, 1996.

The Shaman as Facilitator of Transformation
Hillman, James. *The Soul's Code: In Search of Character and Calling*. New York: Warner Books, 1997.

Kenton, Leslie. *Journey to Freedom: 13 Quantum Leaps for the Soul.* London: Thorsons, 1999.

Mindell, Arnold. *The Shaman's Body: A New Shamanism for Transforming Health, Relationships, and the Community.* New York: HarperSanFrancisco, 1993.

The Shaman as Shape-Shifter
Jamal, Michele. *Deerdancer: The Shapeshifter Archetype in Story and in Trance.* New York: Penguin Arkana, 1995.

Perkins, John. *Shapeshifting: Shamanic Techniques for Global and Personal Transformation.* Rochester, VT: Destiny Books, 1997.

The Shaman as Spiritual Practitioner
Cowan, Tom. *Shamanism as a Spiritual Practice for Daily Life.* Freedom, CA: The Crossing Press, 1996.

Harner, Michael. *The Way of the Shaman.* New York: HarperSanFrancisco, 1990.

The Shaman as Ritual Leader
Braybrooke, Marcus. *Learn to Pray: A Practical Guide to Faith and Inspiration.* San Francisco: Chronicle Books, 2001.

Somé, Malidoma Patrice. *Ritual: Power, Healing, and Community.* New York: Penguin USA, 1997.

The Shaman in the Waking World

Rysdyk, Evelyn C. *Modern Shamanic Living: New Explorations of an Ancient Path.* York Beach, ME: Samuel Weiser, Inc., 1999.

Scott, Gini Graham. *The Complete Idiot's Guide to Shamanism.* Indianapolis, IN: Alpha Books, 2002.

Stevens, José, with Lena Stevens. *The Power Path: The Shaman's Way to Success in Business and Life.* Novato, CA: New World Library, 2002.

Telesco, Patricia. *Shaman in a 9 to 5 World.* Freedom, CA: The Crossing Press, 2000.

Whiteley, Richard. *The Corporate Shaman: A Business Fable.* New York: Harper Business, 2002.

These books explore the intersection of modern scientific thought and the Stone Age wisdom of shamanism.

Bentov, Itzhak. *Stalking the Wild Pendulum: On the Mechanics of Consciousness.* Rochester, VT: Inner Traditions International, 1988.

Brody, Hugh. *The Other Side of Eden: Hunters, Farmers, and the Shaping of the World.* New York: North Point Press, 2002.

McTaggart, Lynne. *The Field: The Quest for the Secret Force of the Universe.* New York: HarperCollins, 2002.

Radin, Dean. *The Conscious Universe: The Scientific Truth of Psychic Phenomena.* New York: HarperSanFrancisco, 1997.

These books offer some interesting cross-cultural influences on contemporary shamanism.

Heinze, Ruth-Inge, *Shamans of the 20th Century.* New York: Irvington Publishers, 1990. *Out of print.*

King, Serge Kahili. *Urban Shaman: A Handbook for Personal and Planetary Transformation Based on the Hawaiian Way of the Adventurer.* New York: Fireside, 1990.

Magee, Matthew. *Peruvian Shamanism: The Pachakúti Mesa.* Chelmsford, MA: Middle Field Publications, 2002.

Sarangerel. *Chosen by the Spirits: Following Your Shamanic Calling.* Rochester, VT: Destiny Books, 2001.

Sarangerel. *Riding Windhorses: A Journey into the Heart of Mongolian Shamanism.* Rochester, VT: Destiny Books, 2000.

Vitebsky, Piers. *The Shaman: Voyages of the Soul Trance, Ecstasy, and Healing from Siberia to the Amazon.* Boston: Little, Brown and Company, 1995.

Wilcox, Joan Parisi. *Keepers of the Ancient Knowledge: The Mystical World of the Q'ero Indians of Peru.* Boston: Sterling Publications, 2002.

Shamanic Journeying

The best recordings for taking shamanic journeys are Michael Harner's series produced by the Foundation for Shamanic Studies. There are many recordings in this series, but I recommend *Solo and Double Drumming, Multiple Drumming,* and *Rattle.* They are available by mail through the Foundation for Shamanic Studies, P.O. Box 1939, Mill Valley, CA, 94942 (415-380-8282), or through their Web site at www.shamanism.org.

About the Author

Tom Crockett is a writer, teacher, and shamanic counselor. Tom currently directs the Institute for Urban Contemporary Shamanism in Newport News, Virginia, where he also maintains a private shamanic counseling practice. He has developed and adapted a form of urban contemporary shamanic practice synthesized from the traditions he has studied. Tom teaches workshops and apprenticeship programs with an emphasis on the contemporary roles of the shamanic practitioner. He is the editor of *Maskan: A Newsletter of Urban Contemporary Shamanism* and the author of *The Artist Inside: A Spiritual Guide to Cultivating Your Creative Self* (Broadway Books, 2000), which explores the idea of the shaman as artist.

Between 1997 and 2001, Tom founded and directed *ArtQuest,* a multicultural arts-based mentoring program at the Hermitage Foundation in Norfolk, Virginia. This program for area high school students uses art and ceremony as a kind of urban tribal initiation program. Through Ancient Wisdom for the New Millennium, Tom leads retreat workshops and experiential journeys in Oaxaca, Mexico, with psychotherapist and Alchemical Dreamwork expert Sven Doehner.

Tom is a summa cum laude graduate of Old Dominion University in Norfolk, Virginia, with a bachelor of fine arts degree. His master of fine arts is from the School of the Art Institute of Chicago. He is an ordained minister of the Circle of the Sacred Earth and the Universal Life Church and he is a member of both the Foundation for Shamanic Studies and the Association for the Study of Dreams.

Tom can be reached through his E-mail address at urbanshaman@cox.net.